"I am pleased to see the public⸱ Lenten season. Each week of ⸱ our stories through the exper died and were brought back to ⸱⸱⸱⸱⸱⸱⸱⸱⸱⸱ ⸱⸱⸱⸱⸱⸱⸱⸱⸱⸱⸱ as each account foreshadows the death and resurrection of Jesus, who is the seventh resurrection. I commend this book for the encouragement of our hearts as we prepare for Easter during Lent."

Andy Chambers, Provost and
Senior Vice President for Academic Affairs
Missouri Baptist University

"Hope! The resurrection of Jesus is all about hope. It becomes even more so when we see traced for us in the pages of Scripture how God has moved in individual lives giving moments of hope in despair. *The Seventh Resurrection* traces those moments of despair turned to hope, all culminating in the ultimate gift of compassion and hope, the resurrection of Jesus! This devotional is powerful and hope-filled, a 'must have' for anyone seeking hope!"

Chad Hodges, Director of Missions
Jefferson Baptist Association

"Every Christian knows the importance of Easter Sunday, but how many Christians prepare their hearts for this important celebration? *The Seventh Resurrection* is a gift to the church, skillfully guiding God's people through the Scriptures and preparing them to experience Resurrection Sunday with fresh eyes and a renewed spirit. This little book will bless you and your church!"

Jeremy Muniz, Senior Pastor
Ridgecrest Baptist Church, Springfield, MO

"*The Seventh Resurrection* gives the reader an emotional spark through articulated stories and, at the same time, edification through sound exegesis of biblical text. The authors write in a concise and relatable fashion that will give any individual depth during the resurrection season."

David Evans, Senior Pastor
Springfield Baptist Church, Springfield, TN

"Daniel Carr and Martin Winslow continue to provide thoughtful and practical devotional insights into God's word with *The Seventh Resurrection*. Like their Advent devotional, *The Seventh Birthday*, this new work draws deeply from the Old Testament as its narrative and prophecies point to the coming Messiah and his resurrection from the dead. *The Seventh Resurrection* is an excellent resource that shows Christ's glorious victory over Satan, sin, and death was anticipated long before the Word became flesh (John 1:14)."

Rob Phillips, Director of Ministry Support & Apologetics
Missouri Baptist Convention

"With engaging stories and careful examination of the Bible, *The Seventh Resurrection* explores six miracles where someone was brought back to life, culminating in the seventh account of Jesus' own resurrection. Like a musical piece that rises to the grand climax, these miracles build in excitement to the moment where Jesus walks out of his grave. The authors beautifully portray the uniqueness of Jesus' resurrection and the practical implications for our lives today as they encourage readers to respond in wonder and worship. *The Seventh Resurrection* highlights the hope we have as Christians: Because Jesus lives, we will also live in glorified bodies, never to die again! This is a fantastic resource for churches and individuals alike."

Heather Kaufman, Author

THE SEVENTH RESURRECTION

BY DANIEL CARR AND MARTIN WINSLOW

Paperback ISBN: 978-1-958988-03-9
Hardcover ISBN: 978-1-958988-04-6
eBook ISBN: 978-1-958988-05-3

HSP Production Team
Executive editor: John Yeats
Editor: Gary Ledbetter
Cover design: Katie Shull
Interior graphics: Tony Boes
Layout: Brandon Benefield
Production management: Gary Ledbetter
Electronic production: Brianna Boes

High Street Press is the publishing arm of the Missouri Baptist Convention (MBC) and exists because of the generous support of Missouri Baptists through the Cooperative Program. To learn more about the MBC and the way 1,800 affiliated churches cooperate voluntarily for the sake of the gospel, visit mobaptist.org. To learn more about High Street Press, visit highstreet.press.

TABLE OF CONTENTS

Introduction   9

Resurrection 1: Son of the Widow at Zarephath   11

Resurrection 2: Son of the Shunammite Woman   27

Resurrection 3: The Israelite Man   45

Resurrection 4: Son of the Widow at Nain   59

Resurrection 5: The Daughter of Jairus   77

Resurrection 6: Lazarus   91

Resurrection 7: Jesus' Resurrection   109

Appendixes   123

INTRODUCTION

Every year on the first Sunday following the full moon, on or just after the spring equinox, Christians celebrate Easter – or, as we prefer, Resurrection Sunday. But what if we told you that there were six other special moments prior to Jesus' resurrection where someone who had died came back to life by God's power through one of his servants?

Throughout biblical history there were several epochs where God empowered specific people with the ability to perform supernatural miracles. We see Moses perform such miraculous signs as turning the Nile River into blood, parting the Red Sea, and casting down his rod and it becoming a serpent. His successor, Joshua, also parted the Jordan River as God's people crossed into the promised land on dry ground. Later, both Elijah and his successor, Elisha, raised the dead (we'll look at these), and caused the rain to stop and then re-start seven years later. Then, of course, Jesus and his apostles performed numerous miraculous signs that defied the normal physical laws of the creation.

As many phenomenal acts of wonder as the servants of God performed, none seem greater than the conquering of death to bring back life. From the Old Testament to the Gospels, we see six death-defeating moments when God's servants brought someone back from the dead. All these remarkable moments point towards the ultimate victory over death – the resurrection of Jesus. On the front end, we do want to address a simple but profound issue. We are referring to all of these as resurrections in the sense that all these events involved people who physically died and then were brought back to life. However, as readers will see near the end, there is really and truly only one resurrection to date. The six people we'll examine in this book were actually resuscitations since each one of them would die again. However, Jesus rose from the dead for all of eternity, as all believers will in the future. So, while we acknowledge that in the truest sense, there has only been one true resurrection to eternity, we refer to the others as resurrections back to the temporal life.

In *The Seventh Resurrection* we want to journey with you through these six miraculous episodes of God overcoming death to prepare you for the glorious event of Easter. We will spend six days with each event, delving into the excitement, hope, and power of each of these events as they foreshadow Jesus' resurrection. With each resurrection event we will focus on one Easter theme. The design of this book is for readers to utilize this study during the season of Lent as we prepare for Easter. We encourage the reader to begin with Day 1 on the Monday before Ash Wednesday and then read one entry per day, EXCEPT SUNDAYS, up through the day before Easter. Each day will include some questions to ponder and proposed prayer to encourage your time with the Lord. The following chart depicts the layout of this book:

Event	Scripture Passage	Servant of God Involved	Easter Theme
1. Son of the Widow at Zarephath	1 Kings 17:8-24	The Prophet Elijah	Faithfulness
2. Son of the Shunammite Woman	2 Kings 4:18-39	The Prophet Elisha	Hope
3. The Israelite Man	2 Kings 13:20-21	The Prophet Elisha	Power
4. Son of the Widow at Nain	Luke 7:11-17	Jesus	Compassion
5. The Daughter of Jairus	Luke 8:49-56	Jesus	Faith
6. Lazarus	John 11:1-44	Jesus	Certainty
7. Jesus' Resurrection	John 20:1-18	Jesus	Victory

Resurrection 1

SON OF THE WIDOW AT ZAREPHATH

1 Kings 17:8-24

DAY 1

Look, I have commanded a woman who is a widow to provide for you there (1 Kings 17:9).

Famine

In January 2010, a massive earthquake struck the small half-island nation of Haiti. The devastation was all but inexpressible. Thousands of people died and thousands more were displaced and left homeless. I (Daniel) was part of a team that traveled to Haiti shortly afterward to assist in any way we could. We partnered with a ministry that donated simple brick-making machines and trained the local workers on how to use them in order to greatly aid in the rebuilding process. However, we also connected with a local orphanage that was overwhelmed due to the many children who had lost their parents in the earthquake. The orphanage was in a house just south of the capital, Port-au-Prince. The first day we arrived at the orphanage absolutely broke my heart. Normally when we've visited orphanages, we would be greeted with dozens of children running up to us with smiles, excitement, and joy. Such was not the case on this April day.

These children were lying on benches, floors, and bare mattresses. They had no smiles, no joy, and all but no hope. And I noticed something else – bloated stomachs. I quickly learned that these children only received two or three meals a week. Their little bodies were trying to compensate for their hunger. We talked with the caretaker, who himself was very thin and gaunt. He led us to the kitchen and pointed to their "rice tub." It was empty. He said, "We haven't eaten in three days." His next words surprised me and humbled me. He said with sincere regret, "I am so sorry that we cannot feed you and your team." In his suffering, stress, and concern for the orphans, he was also greatly concerned for his hospitality to us.

Beyond Possibility

In this biblical account of Elijah, the Bible says that God had already commanded this certain widow to take care of Elijah when he arrived in the village of Zarephath. Her crisis came as the land was in the midst of a severe famine, brought on by God himself as a consequence for King Ahab and Queen Jezebel's wicked disobedience to God. Food and water were scarce.

As Elijah arrived at the widow's home, he asked for a drink of water. She promptly moved to get him some water. Being a time of famine, we assume there was a shortage of water. Her eager response to getting Elijah water demonstrated her incredible hospitality – especially in the face of its scarcity. But his next request went beyond scarce to impossible.

Before she is able to get the water, Elijah also asks, "Please bring me a piece of bread in your hand" (1 Kings 17:11). This request for bread went far beyond any ability this widow had to fulfill. She had no bread. She only had a little flour and a little oil left.

Beyond Hope?
Then this faithful widow reveals more about her view of her own predicament. She confesses to Elijah that she is gathering sticks so she and her son can eat their last little bit of food and then die together, since no more food was available. She had given up, BUT she was still trying to be faithful to God's command to the best of her ability.

Have you found yourself there lately? You've exhausted all your ideas and solutions to try to overcome a real dilemma, but to no avail? You have a desire to be faithful to God, but it just seems impossible at times? For you, it probably isn't food, but have you been trying to overcome an addictive habit? Restore a marriage? Reconcile with a betrayed friend? Tried to regain a job you lost? Stay pure in a relationship?

You're not alone. Genuine faith picks up when we come to the end of our ability. God often calls us to do things that are beyond our reach – beyond our capacity. Just as he commanded this widow to feed Elijah out of nothing, he calls us to follow him out of our emptiness.

The good news is that God knows this AND he wants you to be able to obey and follow him. As we'll see in tomorrow's reading, God uses Elijah to help the widow obey. As for the orphanage, God had sent our team to help them obey and be hospitable to us. We went and bought them food for three months – rice, vegetables, chickens, goats, and fruits. What a glorious day to see them then be excited to cook for us – and even more – to see those hungry children eat to their hearts' content.

God will supply what you need to obey. He wants you to trust him. So, whatever impossibility you may be facing today, trust him. After all, if Jesus conquered death, enabling you to conquer your inability to be obedient is definitely within his ability.

Questions for Day 1
1. If you were the widow and God told you to take care of Elijah when you had nothing, what would be your response?

2. Why would God give this widow a command that she did not have the means to obey?
3. What is something God has called you to do that, at first, you didn't think there was any way you could do?
4. What do you need to trust God for today?

Prayer for Day 1
God, remind us today that nothing is too difficult for you. Lord, please continue to show me that when you call me to do something, you always want me to be successful in obedience and you will provide the way for me to be obedient. Please help me trust you more.

DAY 2
FAITHFUL SUSTAINMENT

The flour jar did not become empty, and the oil jug did not run dry…
(1 Kings 17:16a).

Nothing Left
In a church I (Daniel) pastored in Tennessee, we had an elder who shared his and his wife's story about their journey to learning generosity. He told of how, early in their marriage, shortly after they had become followers of Jesus, God had convicted them of his desire for them to learn how to be generous. So he and his wife decided to start tithing to the local church. Within a week of their new commitment to Jesus, he lost his job. Yet, he and his wife committed to maintain the same level of giving as if he had been employed. As he told the story, he admitted that there was no command that said he had to maintain that level of giving, but that he and his wife believed the Lord was teaching them to trust him. Weeks went by and he was not able to secure a job. Weeks became months. One day his wife broke down. "We don't even have enough money for toilet paper!" she cried. At this point, the man telling the story said with a tear in his eye, "I have never felt like such a failure." He recounted how he and his wife prayed and decided to keep trusting the Lord for his provision. That afternoon, he checked the mail. When he discovered the contents in the mailbox he leapt with joy and laughter. He ran inside to show his wife what they had received in the mailbox – a roll of toilet paper. A company had been placing free samples in the neighborhood's mailboxes as an advertisement campaign. But this couple knew God was behind even such small details as these.

At the End of Ourselves
In 1 Kings 17, the widow at Zarephath finds herself in dire straits. She only has enough oil and flour for one more small meal for her son and herself. In her mind, there is no logical way she can also feed Elijah. She is prepared to eat this last meal and then die with her son. But God had other plans. So often, when we are at the end of our abilities, our solutions, our ideas – God steps in and does his greatest work.

Elijah told her to go back and cook what she had, making him a cake first, and then to make some for her son and herself because God was supernaturally not going to allow her jar of flour or her jug of oil to empty until the rains returned. Was this a test? Could she trust Elijah and this word from the Lord? This just did not make sense. How could this happen?

A genuine faith believes and trusts in God when our solutions and ideas have fallen far short. This is why Proverbs 3:5-6 says, "Trust in the LORD with all your heart, and do not lean on your own understanding. In all your ways acknowledge him, and he will make straight your paths."

Supernatural Provision

This widow decided to trust in the Lord and his prophet Elijah, and did what Elijah had instructed. As a result of her faith and God's merciful provision, this widow and her son had plenty to feed themselves and Elijah for the duration of the famine. She was faithful and hospitable because of the provision of God.

Are you at the end of yourself? Do you see no way forward, no rational solution, or little hope? Take heart. God is on his throne and loves to do what only he can do.

After our friends found the toilet paper in their mailbox, good news continued to roll in. He decided to go into business for himself, along with a partner. Years later, they continue to thrive in their business and in their relationship with Christ – and they are some of the most generous people I've ever met.

Don't worry. There is the other side of this in your life, too. God will do something. He will move, answer, and provide. As Jesus said, "But seek first his kingdom and his righteousness, and all these things will be given to you as well" (Matthew 6:33).

Questions for Day 2

1. If you were the widow, why would you be able to trust what Elijah was telling you?
2. Describe a time when you felt helpless to give aid to someone that you really wanted to help.
3. Are you currently at the end of yourself in a particular circumstance or situation? How can you place your trust and confidence in God's provision?
4. What is a story from your faith journey of trusting in God to provide and him doing so?

Prayer for Day 2

Lord God, you are the one who created everything. You are all-powerful and almighty. You also love us with a perfect love. Thank you for caring for me more than I can understand. Help me to trust you even in the times when it seems all hope is gone and I have no solution. Lord, you are completely trustworthy and faithful. Increase my faith.

DAY 3
FAITHFUL AMIDST DOUBT

She said to Elijah, "What have you against me, O man of God?"
(1 Kings 17:18).

The Burden of Doubt
In my (Daniel) early days in the army, I had a friend who carried a heavy burden of doubt. He had grown up in church. He had been a part of a collegiate Christian campus ministry with me. We had spent hours praying together, studying together, and worshiping together. Yet, in those early days of adulthood he struggled with a heavy doubt about whether God had truly forgiven him of his past. This doubt caused my army buddy numerous sleepless nights and a higher level of stress than a person should have in his life. Was God against him? Doubt can wreak havoc in our lives, especially in those seasons when we doubt God's love for us or his willingness to forgive us.

A Drastic Change of Direction
The widow of Zarephath had been so blessed to experience a true miracle of God. She had watched as her jar of flour and jug of oil did not run dry despite months of daily use. Oh, how kind God was to her! But suddenly, her son became very ill to the point where "no breath remained in him" (17). What happened? Why this sudden and violent turn of events?

The Scripture does not reveal what had happened to her husband or how long she had been a widow. However, one can easily surmise that her son was her only family in the world. No doubt, as with most mothers, her only child was her life! Immediately, doubt flooded into her soul. She turns to Elijah – the man who had been the instrument of rescue and deliverance from starvation – and she now views him as the instrument of wrath, sickness, and even death. "What have you against me, O man of God?" she asks. What had she done? Why was God angry? Why was Elijah angry?

Choosing Faith
What did this suffering widow do with her doubt? Did she run from God? Curse God and abandon hope in him? No. She made the "not so easy" decision to trust in God and his man Elijah regardless of her doubt. She entrusted her son to Elijah and the Lord.

As my friend in the army continued to struggle with his doubt, we finally contacted our pastor at the time, who graciously met us for lunch. My friend unloaded his burdens to the pastor, who listened intently. When my friend finished, the pastor responded, "The fact that you're so worried about it is strong evidence you are truly a believer. My counsel to you is to continue to obey the Lord. Continue to serve the Lord. Continue to worship him and fellowship with his people. He'll take care of the rest." And you know what? God did. He really took care of the rest. Within a month the stress my buddy had experienced vanished and, instead, he had a confident walk with Jesus – and still does to this day.

Are you in a season of wrestling with doubt? Has your life seemingly taken a drastic turn? Don't let your doubts overtake you. Don't buy into the thoughts of despair. Take a cue from this widow who thought her world was crumbling. But she decided to still trust in God.

Questions for Day 3
1. Who else do we know of in the Bible that wrestled with doubt? How did they handle it?
2. When her child became critically ill, who does it seem that she blamed?
3. How have you wrestled with doubt in God's love and forgiveness?
4. What does it look like for you to trust in God right now, despite any doubt you may have?

Prayer for Day 3
O Lord! You are always faithful, even in the midst of our doubts. Lord, make my faith in you stronger. Help me to trust in you beyond my doubts. Forgive me in those seasons of doubt. In your grace, please allow me to see you working in my life and in the lives of others today. Thank you for your forgiveness and the privilege of being a part of your kingdom.

DAY 4
FAITHFUL IN DESPERATION

But Elijah said to her, "Give me your son." So he took him from her arms, brought him up to the upstairs room (1 Kings 17:19).

The Motivation of Desperation
In 1963, a middle-aged Mary Kay Ash sat alone, depressed, and jobless. Recently widowed (her husband had suddenly collapsed and died from a heart attack), and alienated from a male-dominated workplace, she would later say, "I lived across the street from a mortuary, and I began to wonder if I should call them up and tell them to 'come on over.'"[1] She had no income and very little savings in the bank. What would she do?

This devastated widow of Zarephath found herself in that tragic moment of losing her only child – and probably the only family she had. She has just demonstrated some level of doubt in the intentions of the man of God, Elijah himself. Now, as she holds the body of her dearest love in her arms, she is all but at the end of hope.

Just a Mustard Seed
Jesus says, "if you have faith like a grain of mustard seed, you'll say to this mountain, 'Move from here to there,' and it will move, and nothing will be impossible for you" (Matthew 17:20b). Jesus' point is that even just a little faith is powerful. As this widow hopelessly holds the body of her breathless son, Elijah takes the boy's body from her arms and proceeds upstairs. How does the widow respond? Does she demand her son's body back? Does she exclaim out of pain and anger, "Haven't you already brought enough calamity on me?"

No. Despite her doubts and her devastation, she has at least a mustard seed of faith. She has seen enough evidence of God's power through Elijah that she still dares to believe, even in the face of such ardent desperation. Could Elijah, whom God had used to sustain them through the famine, now do something unheard of in the face of the death of her son? She watches with a little hope and a little faith as Elijah carries her beloved boy's body up the stairs. But a little is all she needs.

Faith U-Turns
The Bible is full of historical accounts when God acts in a way that takes someone who has nearly bottomed out in faith and turns them around. This widow had just bottomed out with the dying of her son. But what God was about to do would turn her faith and her life around.

Nearly at the end of herself, Mary Kay Ash managed to gather her strength and, with faith, launched Mary Kay Cosmetics. The company grew to become a $2.5 billion enterprise that provided numerous women inspiration, jobs, and satisfaction.[2] What about you? Have you bottomed out in any way? Are you finding yourself desperate, at the end of hope? All you need is that mustard seed of faith. Hang on! Trust in God even when things seem impossible – because with him, nothing is impossible.

Questions for Day 4

1. Do you remember a moment of desperation in your life? How did you respond?
2. Do you think, if you were the widow, you would have allowed Elijah to carry off your son?
3. When have you trusted in the Lord with something that seemed impossible?

Prayer for Day 4

Lord, I praise you that you are the God over the impossible! I pray you increase my faith. Thank you for how you've shown me evidence of your faithfulness in Scripture and in my life. When I feel like I'm losing hope, remind me of your presence and your faithfulness.

Daddy, Daddy, Daddy – DANIEL!

I (Daniel) love being a dad. I have seven kids and they are so much fun and bring so much joy to my life. I have learned so much about God as my Father from being a dad myself. One such joy is always having a house full of life, jokes, laughs, mischief, and NOISE! As a dad, and an inhabitant of a house with nine people, one grows eerily accustomed to loudness. Amazingly, God gives us the ability to move the noise to the background after time so we can still maintain our sanity in the midst of continuous high-decibel levels. However, the downside of that is when one of your sweet little image-bearers needs your attention. Their call for you can be drowned out by the other noise, or unnoticed as their call just blends in with the white noise of loudness to which you've grown accustomed.

I've often laughed at this until recently. My youngest son was trying to get my attention. He is a fresh six years old. He had undoubtedly been saying, "Daddy!" for a couple of minutes. Finally, in a last-ditch effort to grab my attention, my six-year-old exclaimed, "DANIEL!" I finally heard him. I was struck with a conviction that I am not the listener I should be for the voices of my children. I am so thankful that God is a much better listener to his kids than I am.

The Ear That Hears

Once Elijah took the dead boy out of the arms of his mother – the widow at Zarephath – he took the boy upstairs and cried out to God. In fact, the Bible says here that he cried out to God twice – once asking God why, and once pleading for God to restore life to the boy. Then, there is one of the most amazing phrases in all the Bible: "And the LORD listened to the voice of Elijah" (1 Kings 17:22).

We cannot imagine all that God hears at any given moment. We know at any given instant, millions of people are praying to him. The Bible also says such voices call out to him as the blood of the slain like Abel (Genesis 4), creation "pours out speech" (Psalm 19:2), angels constantly repeat "Holy, holy, holy" (Isaiah 6), and countless other sounds and words from myriads of sources resound. Yet, as one scans the Scriptures, one sees that at no time does God fail to listen to anyone who cries out to him. As the psalmist writes, "a broken and contrite heart, O God, you will not despise" (Psalm 51:7). And Isaiah records, "But this is the one to whom I look: he who is humble and contrite in spirit and trembles at my word" (Isaiah 66:2b). In a way we cannot fathom, God hears our cries to him. He listens!

The God Who Answers
God responds to Elijah's cry. He restores. When David cried out to God in Psalm 51, God forgave. When Moses cried out to God at the edge of the Red Sea fleeing from the Egyptians, God listened and responded by parting the water. God listens and he responds according to his will.

I will never forget God's answer to the prayers of our church back in 2003. My second daughter had just turned one. The pediatrician had shown significant concern for her as she had what the doctor referred to as a "clicking hip." The doctor described her condition as having an underdeveloped hip socket with a high probability she would not crawl or walk – perhaps ever. Sure enough, on her first birthday, she still was not even crawling.

At the end of a church service in our church plant, I asked for the church to pray for our daughter. That beautiful small congregation of young Christians – without my prompting – proceeded to get up from their seats and come forward to pray for my daughter Rachelle. Now there wasn't any earthquake or rocks splitting, just heart-felt and love-driven prayer. We went home, thankful and encouraged by the prayers of God's people. But honestly, we did not have an expectation that God was going to respond. Oh, we of little faith. The next morning, we got our daughter out of her crib and laid her on the floor so she could roll around and be active. I turned my back on her to get some items off the changing table and, when I turned around, there she was crawling out her bedroom door for the first time. I just stared with tear-filled eyes and stood in awe that God not only listened to his sweet people in that little church plant – but he answered.

God hears you. God listens to your voice. Grab his ear in your desperation, in the cries of your heart with confidence knowing that amidst all the noise of the universe, your cry bursts through to the ear and heart of our heavenly Father.

Questions for Day 5
1. Does it surprise you that God listens to your prayers? Why or why not?
2. Does God owe us his attention?
3. What is a story you can share of when God answered your prayer?
4. What are you crying out to the Lord for right now?

Prayer for Day 5

Heavenly Father, I am overwhelmed today by the simply incredible truth that you hear my prayer. Thank you for being the perfect Father who always listens and answers according to your will. Lord, I cry out to you today for _____.

DAY 6
FAITHFUL POWER

*… and the boy's life came into him again, and he lived
(1 Kings 17:22b).*

Defining Moments
Everyone has those moments in life that are not only unforgettable, but also actually change us and shape us from that day forward. These moments steer our lives in a new direction. Our faith is greatly impacted. Our perspective becomes much more focused and more in tune with the Lord. Perhaps what you did not even consider a possibility suddenly took center stage of your life. Like David going from being just a runt shepherd boy to being the hero of Israel who killed Goliath. Or Paul who went from being a notorious hater of the church to being one of her greatest leaders once he met Jesus. A few moments can define our lives.

No Precedent
As Elijah carried the boy's body upstairs, it is hard not to ponder what the widow at Zarephath was thinking. If, indeed, the thought crossed her mind that perhaps Elijah could raise him from the dead, the very fact that she had that thought would be miraculous. There was no precedent for such a thought. No one in all of history had been brought back from the dead by God or one of his prophets prior to this moment. She had no story or biblical example from which to draw hope. She had very little to no theological framework from which to draw such a hopeful concept. Neither did Elijah.

Elijah pleaded with God to restore this boy's life to him (1 Kings 17:21). Even though that had never before happened, Elijah had seen God do the supernatural on numerous occasions, such as with the oil and flour. He had also seen God close up the heavens and withhold rain for three and a half years. He would later see God's power release the heavens again and let the rain fall. He saw enough evidence of God to reinforce all he knew God had done for his people earlier. All of this greatly bolstered the faith of Elijah.

Power of God on Display
God answered the cries of Elijah. He restored life to the boy. Can you imagine? Did the boy suddenly gasp for air? Did he cough and sputter? Did he simply open his eyes and say something humorous to Elijah? Regardless, this was a defining moment for Elijah, the widow, and the boy. Elijah would go down as one of the very few humans that God used to raise someone from the dead. The widow is forever

known as the mother of the boy raised from the dead. And the boy? Jewish tradition taught by rabbis for centuries holds that the boy is none other than the prophet Jonah.[1] If that is true, no wonder he knew God could forgive and restore Nineveh. If God had raised him from the dead, what couldn't God do?

In theology, we talk about the attributes of God. One such attribute is God's omnipotence, which means he is all-powerful. He created the entire cosmos with the spoken word (Genesis 1). He holds the universe together (Colossians 1:17). All of creation proclaims his glory (Psalm 19:1). Regardless of what is going on in your life or in our world – nothing is beyond the power of Almighty God. ABSOLUTELY NOTHING!

Questions for Day 6
1. What would you have done if you were there and saw the boy come back to life?
2. What has God done in your life that you never even expected?
3. In what area of your life do you need God's power the most? Pray and ask him.
4. What about our nation or world makes you feel the most hopeless? Pray for God to do the impossible.

Prayer for Day 6
Lord, I believe you are all-powerful. I believe you raised the dead – especially Jesus to save us from our lostness. Father, I pray you would show your power in my life. I pray for you to reveal your power in our nation and in our world.

Notes for Resurrection 1: Son of the Widow at Zarephath

Day 4
[1] Greg Satell, May 8, 2011. https://digitaltonto.com/2011/triumphant-tales-of-heartbreaking-desperation/.
[2] Ibid.

Day 6
[1] Keil and Delitzsh, *Biblical Commentary on the Old Testament: Jonah*, electronic version. https://www.sacred-texts.com/bib/cmt/kad/jon000.htm.

Resurrection 2

SON OF THE SHUNAMMITE WOMAN

2 Kings 4:18-39

DAY 7
HOPING TO BLESS

Let us make a small room on the roof with walls and put there for him a bed, a table, a chair, and a lamp so that whenever he comes to us, he can go in there (2 Kings 4:10).

The Gift of Hospitality

I (Martin) love hospitality, don't you? For some people the gift of hospitality seems so natural, doesn't it? They can easily find a way to make you feel at home and loved. In a little bitty village off the beaten path in Senegal, Africa, I have received some of the best hospitality that I could ever imagine. This hospitality is provided from a tribe of Fulani Muslims. This small dusty village, out in the bush, is called Gurel. There, in this unassuming village, you will meet some of the kindest people anywhere. These African friends of mine give every American a new African name. Mine is Samba Ba! They have adopted our American group into their people and have even become very open to the gospel through the years.

In American culture it is typical to greet someone with the words, "What's up?" or "How are you doing?" It is a general question that expects a general answer. The greeting of my friends in this village goes like this:

"Hono sukaabe maa?"
    "How are your children?"

"Hono nay maa?"
    "How are your cows?"

"Hono baali maa?"
    "How are your sheep?"

"Hono bey maa?"
    "How are your goats?"

"Hono ndunngu o?"
    "How was rainy season?"

"Hono ceedu o?"
    "How was dry season?"

"Mi yeewniima sehhilam!"
    "I have missed you, my friend!"

After the greeting and a few hugs, comes the sit down with these friends and the drinking of *attaya* – hot tea filled with too much sugar! Incredible hospitality! Even though these friends of mine don't know the saving power of Jesus, they certainly know the power of good hospitality.

In days 7-12 we will look carefully at the story of Elisha raising the Shunammite's son from the dead. This story starts off with the Shunammite woman hoping to bless Elisha with her gift of hospitality. The story ends with Elisha hoping to bless back the Shunammite by God performing the miracle of resurrection through him.

Leveraging Wealth for Others

The city of Shunem must have had hospitality much like that of the little village I visit in Senegal. When the wealthy Shunammite woman saw that Elisha was passing through her town, she quickly decided that her gift could meet his need by feeding him each time he passed through the area (2 Kings 4:8). She went on to tell her husband that she believed that Elisha was a holy man of God. Because of this, she said to her husband, "Let us make a small room on the roof with walls and put there for him a bed, a table, a chair, and a lamp, so that whenever he comes to us, he can go in there."

Notice that Elisha doesn't ask for this blessing from the woman. She offers the blessing because she discerns the need. In ancient Israel, God makes it clear that hospitality is very important. Ezekiel 16:49 says, "'Now this was the sin of your sister Sodom: She and her daughters were arrogant, overfed and unconcerned; they did not help the poor and needy." In the book of 1 Peter we read, "Show hospitality to one another without grumbling." When people are hospitable, they demonstrate that their belongings don't belong to them, but to God. When we meet the Shunammite woman, it is clear that her desire to bless Elisha was a natural outworking of her God-given gift.

So... What Now?

It's important for Christians to not only read and learn but also to apply. Elisha was a man on a mission from God. He received the mantle of a prophet from his predecessor Elijah. He preached righteousness to Israel and worked miracles by the power of God. His ministry was critical, and the Shunammite woman recognized it. Because of this, she leveraged her wealth to join God in what he was doing. How are you doing this with your finances and/or hospitality? When I think of my experiences in Senegal and I read about the Shunammite, I realize that there is a lot to learn from these dusty little towns.

Questions for Day 7

1. Romans 12:13 says, "Contribute to the needs of the saints and seek to show hospitality." How does your family seek to do this?
2. Who do you know that has the natural gift of hospitality?
3. How has someone impacted you through their gift of hospitality?
4. Is there anything that your family can do to show a neighbor hospitality?

Prayer for Day 7

Father, thank you for providing for me all that you have given me. You are the ultimate picture of hospitality. Everything that I have is from you and I recognize that today. Please help me to learn from the Shunammite's example of recognizing where you are at work.

DAY 8
HOPE AND FEAR

And he said, "At this season, about this time next year, you shall embrace a son." And she said, "No, my lord, O man of God; do not lie to your servant" (2 Kings 4:16).

Do You Hope or Fear?

Are you a glass half-empty or half-full type of a person? An optimist, a pessimist, or are you one of those who just calls yourself a realist? When the chips are down in a situation, do you find yourself hopeful or quickly waving the white flag of defeat? Maybe you have found yourself in a very hopeful spot in life in the past only to see your hopes dashed and your prayers seemingly unanswered. Perhaps you worked hard for a promotion only to see someone else elevated above you. Maybe someone else received the college scholarship that you worked for and thought you deserved.

Several disappointments in a row can lead to an overwhelming feeling of hopelessness. If you have ever had a streak of negative things happen to you in the past, it can be hard to believe that things may turn around in your future. We must be careful to not allow the disappointments from the past to sabotage our futures. As believers, we must remain hopeful people because, ultimately, we know that the God of the Bible is in control. His plan is best, even if we don't understand his decisions.

The Shunammite's Fear

The Shunammite was scared. Elisha told her that something would happen in her life for which she had obviously given up hope. Because of her incredible hospitality, Elisha wanted to bless the Shunammite in return. Elisha speaks through Gehazi because apparently the Shunammite doesn't understand Elisha's language. 2 Kings 4:12-13 says, "And he said to Gehazi his servant, 'Call this Shunammite.' When he had called her, she stood before him. And he said to him, 'Say now to her, "See, you have taken all this trouble for us; what is to be done for you?"'" When Elisha sees that the woman doesn't really have any requests of him, Gehazi tells Elisha the Shunammite has no child, and her husband is old. Elisha speaks to Gehazi, "He said, 'Call her.' And when he had called her, she stood in the doorway. And he said, 'At this season, about this time next year, you shall embrace a son.' And she said, 'No, my lord, O man of God; do not lie to your servant.'"

The Pain of Hope

Just like today and maybe even more so, bearing children in the ancient Near East was very important to a woman. We can see the grieving of Hannah in the first chapter of 1 Samuel as a perfect example of this. She was weeping over her infertility in the tabernacle so fiercely that Eli, the high priest, thought she was drunk (1 Sam. 1:14-15). The pain of infertility has caused this grieving to come to many women through the years. Apparently, the Shunammite was in this same situation. Whether the issue was with her husband, who was old, or with the woman herself, we aren't told. We just know that she had endured mental pain over not being able to conceive. In fact, when Elisha says to her that she is going to have a child, she replies, "do not lie to your servant." Hope in this situation for the Shunammite was a painful thing to have. Instead of hope, she had fear.

Do you have hope or fear when you consider the future? Maybe you are in the middle of cancer treatments, and things aren't looking good for your recovery. Do the promises of God bring you hope, or are you concentrating on the fear of losing this life? Remember what Paul said to the Philippians: "For me to live is Christ, but to die is gain." If you have Jesus Christ, you never have a reason to not be hopeful. Maybe you are barely able to pay your bills, but you must remember, "he has caused us to be born again to a living hope through the resurrection of Jesus Christ from the dead, to an inheritance that is imperishable, undefiled, and unfading, kept in heaven for you" (1 Peter 1:3b-4). Whatever your situation, don't let the fear of your circumstances outweigh the hope you have in Christ.

Questions for Day 8

1. What situation in your life right now is causing you to fear the future? Have you given this situation to the Lord? If so, how so?
2. In what past situations have you seen the Lord work to cause you to hope? Maybe it was a situation where you were fearful, yet God delivered that situation in a mighty way.
3. Can you understand the reluctance of the Shunammite to believe Elisha's prophecy? Why do you think she was so scared?
4. What situations are going on right now in your life that you need to be hopeful about? Do you have fear or hope over these situations?

Prayer for Day 8

Father, help me today to be a hopeful person. Remind me of the times in my life and in the lives of others where you have done miracles. Help me to trust in your power and strength to overcome my fears about the future. I thank you that no matter what happens here on this earth, I have the promise of an inheritance being guarded by Jesus Christ.

DAY 9
HOPE FULFILLED

But the woman conceived, and she bore a son about that time the following spring, as Elisha had said to her (2 Kings 4:17).

Don't Give Up Hope

Kevin Jorgenson had nearly given up all hope of accomplishing his dream. He and climbing partner Tommy Caldwell were striving to become the first to successfully free climb the Dawn Wall of the famous Yosemite mountain, El Capitan. No one had climbed the Dawn Wall before, and it was starting to look like it would remain that way. For six days, Jorgenson had failed the most difficult part of the climb, pitch 15. Caldwell, the more experienced, had quickly gotten past the difficult pitch 15, but Jorgenson was stuck. "There are tiny little holds, but they're far apart and facing different directions,"[1] said Josh Lowell, a filmmaker who had been chronicling the pair's attempts at the Dawn Wall for several years. "Some you grab in awkward ways, sometimes barely by your fingertips, sometimes cocking your wrist in weird angles."[2] Caldwell said that pitch 15 contained "some of the smallest and sharpest holds I have ever attempted to hold onto. It's crazy to think that the skin on our fingertips could be the limiting fact towards success or failure." After six days of failure with the tape and skin ripped off his fingers, Jorgenson finally reached deep and finished pitch 15. After the celebration was over, he and Caldwell finished climbing the Dawn Wall and wrote their names in the record books. Jorgenson is a good reminder that we should never give up.

It's a Boy!

The Shunammite was scared to hope. It would have been easier and less painful to put her dream of having a child behind her. After years of failure at having children, she was clearly afraid to hope again. However, she found out that God can do anything that he wants. This time she would not be disappointed! Just as Elisha had predicted, she conceived, and eventually a little baby boy was born to her. The Scriptures simply say in 2 Kings 4:17, "But the woman conceived, and she bore a son about that time the following spring, as Elisha had said to her." Her dream of having a child had finally come true. Interestingly, we are never told that the Shunammite woman is barren. It seems as though in this situation, the miracle happened for her husband, who Gehazi said was old. Apparently the Shunammite wasn't past normal child-bearing age, but her husband was. The author of Hebrews tells us that in the Old Testament Sarah believed God's promise that she would have a child even though she was past the age of childbearing. Hebrews 11:11 says, "And by faith even Sarah, who was past childbearing age, was enabled to bear children because she considered him faithful who had made the promise." In the case of the Shunammite it seems as though the promise from Elisha enabled her husband to miraculously impregnate his wife rather than for the Shunammite to miraculously conceive. Whatever exactly happened, the Shunammite, just like a barren woman who miraculously conceived, was now a joyous mother of a son.

Hope Fulfilled

Recently I (Martin) rejoiced with a friend over a promotion he received at work. For several years this friend had been passed over while others got promoted around him. Each one of his work reviews through the years was superb. Neither he nor I could figure out why he wasn't being promoted. Time after time he would reinterview with his company hoping to get the higher position, but he would find himself disappointed again and again. In fact, he was so disappointed and discouraged that one day he told me another opening had arisen in the company but he didn't think that he would apply for it. To him it seemed as though it was no use. He had been through the disappointments for so long that he was sure he could predict the outcome. I, along with his family and some other friends, encouraged him to try again. We prayed and trusted that God knew what was best for our friend. This time, my friend's hope was fulfilled. He got the promotion!

The Shunammite and her husband, like my friend, continued to try for that which seemed out of reach. Kevin Jorgenson, at the beginning of our story, did the same thing. Sometimes we fail and never see our prayers answered the way we think that they should be. God is still sovereign and his is the best plan even if we can't understand it. But, like Jorgenson, the Shunammite, and my friend, we should never give up. God may fulfill that hope that we have in our hearts. One of my friends used to say, "If you are praying for potatoes, you better have a hoe in your hand." Keep striving, trust God, swing the hoe, and trust him for the rain.

Questions for Day 9

1. Have you found yourself giving up on something that you believed God wanted you to do? Have you had perseverance in the face of difficulty?
2. What makes us give up hope sometimes?
3. Have you seen a miraculous answer to prayer in your life? Share it with your family or someone close to you.
4. Even when God says no, and your prayers aren't answered the way you think they should be, will you trust him?

Prayer for Day 9

Father, help me to not give up on trusting you. Help this story of the Shunammite to remind me that you can do anything that you want. I pray that you will help me to be diligent inside of your will to trust you for great things. Help me to never give up striving for things that grow your kingdom.

HOPING TO BLESS

And when he had lifted him and brought him to his mother, the child sat on her lap till noon, and then he died (2 Kings 4:20).

March 20, 1995

It's cliché but true: I (Martin) remember it like it was yesterday. A young girl – a close friend – was in her bedroom taking her last breaths while family sadly looked on. At the time I was only 18 years old. To watch a friend passing on and having no way to help was frustrating. Annie Sisk had battled ovarian cancer for over three years. She had multiple surgeries, a bone marrow transplant, and chemotherapy. Everything had failed. Now, as she was entering her final moments, all we could do was weep as we watched her slip into eternity. Annie's mother, Dala (my future mother-in-law), held her daughter for the last time that evening and grieved with grief that no one can understand unless you've been there.

Hope in Tragedy

Everything must have seemed great for the Shunammite and her family. She was wealthy, hospitable to God's prophet, and now her young son was old enough to go into the fields with his father. Then tragedy struck. We aren't told the details of what happened, only of a farming accident that is alluded to in the story. 2 Kings 4:18-20 says, "When the child had grown, he went out one day to his father among the reapers. And he said to his father, 'Oh, my head, my head!' The father said to his servant, 'Carry him to his mother.' And when he had lifted him and brought him to his mother, the child sat on her lap till noon, and then he died."

Instead of beginning to plan the funeral, the Shunammite took her son upstairs and laid him on Elisha's bed. This desperate mother then went out and got a donkey and quickly rode to Mount Carmel to find Elisha. When the Shunammite saw Elisha, she broke tradition and surprised both Gehazi and Elisha by grabbing the feet of the prophet. Gehazi was so startled that he was going to push her away, but Elisha forbade him from doing this. Elisha said to Gehazi in verse 27, "Leave her alone, for she is in bitter distress, and the LORD has hidden it from me and has not told me." While Elisha and Gehazi are both puzzled, she said, "Did I ask my lord for a son?" and didn't I say, "Do not deceive me?" Instantly Elisha figures out that the boy has died! The Shunammite ran to the only man she knew might be able to help – Elisha.

What If?

Maybe you have lost a loved one like our family lost Annie. When you read stories in the Bible about God working miracles, don't you hope in the moment that he will do a miracle and raise your loved one from the dead? It's tempting to think that if Elisha or Jesus were on earth at that moment, maybe we wouldn't have lost Annie. Maybe they would have raised her. At this point in our story, the Shunammite is demonstrating her faith in the fact that she believes Elisha can raise her son from the dead. You can almost picture her holding her son as he took his last breath and thinking, "What if? What if Elisha, whom God used to give me this boy, could also be used by God to raise him?" She rode that donkey as fast as she could to find out the answer to the death of her son.

October 6, 2020

On October 6, 2020, two people were reunited after being apart for 25 years. This special day was when Dala went to see Annie again. This time she wasn't holding Annie's lifeless body. This time she was greeted by her daughter who was found in Christ and would never taste death again. This day in history, Dala got to see her Savior and her saved daughter renewed and full of life. During those 25 years that Dala and Annie were apart, there were lots of conversations about what it was going to be like to see her again. Dala never wavered in her belief that she would one day see her again – not even the day that Annie passed. We serve a Savior that defeated the works of the devil (1 John 3:8). He paid the price for all of our sins and conquered death completely and totally.

Because of the gospel, both Annie and Dala had been brought to life for a second time while they were here on earth. They had both been born again. They had accepted the good news of Jesus and had already experienced the power of resurrection.

> And you, who were dead in your trespasses and the uncircumcision of your flesh, God made alive together with him, having forgiven us all our trespasses, by canceling the record of debt that stood against us with its legal demands. This he set aside, nailing it to the cross. He disarmed the rulers and authorities and put them to open shame, by triumphing over them in him (Colossians 2:13-15).

Have you been brought to life through Christ?

Questions for Day 10

1. Have you ever lost a loved one? Did you have hope on the day of their death or despair?

2. Do you think that if you were the Shunammite you would have run to Elisha for help like she did?
3. Why do you think that the Shunammite believed Elisha could help her?
4. Are you bitter from a past loss of a loved one? Have you trusted that God knows what's right in every situation? Are you comforted by the hope you have in Jesus?
5. Have you trusted in Jesus like Annie and Dala did? Have you been born again and experienced resurrection life in Christ?

Prayer for Day 10
Father, help me to trust you in the day of tragedy. Help me to know that you are near to me and have a plan that is good in every situation. I thank you, God, that through Jesus Christ, you have defeated death and given me eternal life in Christ!

DAY 11
HOPE REALIZED

The child sneezed seven times, and the child opened his eyes. Then he summoned Gehazi and said, "Call this Shunammite." So he called her. And when she came to him, he said, "Pick up your son" (2 Kings 4:35b-36).

The Reality of Hope
Our stories have been building up to this moment. My friend got the promotion and saw hope realized, didn't he? Kevin Jorgenson climbed through pitch 15, conquered the Dawn Wall, and saw hope realized, didn't he? Dala saw her daughter Annie again! She experienced hope realized, didn't she? The Shunammite who was childless conceived and saw hope realized, didn't she? We are people who serve a God who allows us to be hopeful for good reason. The Shunammite knew that Elisha's God could bring her child back from the dead. She sprang to action as quickly as she could and tracked down the prophet to beg for a miracle.

Elisha Springs to Action
Elisha immediately sent Gehazi to run ahead of him and lay Elisha's staff on the boy's face. Verse 31 says, "Gehazi went on ahead and laid the staff on the face of the child, but there was no sound or sign of life. Therefore, he returned to meet him and told him, 'The child has not awakened.'" Elisha followed up by going into the bedroom where the dead boy lay and shutting the door behind him. According to verses 34-35, "Then he went up and lay on the child, putting his mouth on his mouth, his eyes on his eyes, and his hands on his hands. And as he stretched himself upon him, the flesh of the child became warm. Then he got up again and walked once back and forth in the house and went up and stretched himself upon him. The child sneezed seven times, and the child opened his eyes." The boy was raised from the dead!

A Second Miracle
The Shunammite woman knew that the God of Elisha had delivered on his promise to give her a child. She also knew that this same God could give him life a second time. She ran to Elisha because he knew the God who could do this impossible task. It is definitely one of the weirder miracles we see in the Bible. Elisha literally puts his mouth over the dead boy's mouth! However, the Lord used the faith of Elisha to raise this boy from the dead. Neither the Shunammite nor Elisha are

reluctant to have hope in this situation. Both spring to action upon the death of the boy. The Shunammite runs to Elisha and Elisha runs to the house. Both have a hope in the God who answers prayers.

The Bed of Elisha

At the beginning of this story, the Shunammite and her husband bless Elisha by feeding him and building him a small room onto their house with a bed so that the man of God will have a place to rest on his journeys. When the Shunammite's son dies, she lays the boy on the bed with which she had blessed Elijah. I have wondered while reading this story if she is in a way reminding God and Elisha of the blessing that she has been to God's prophet. Why not lay her son on her own bed? She specifically lays her son on Elisha's bed, and the place that she blessed Elisha now becomes the place that blesses her. Elisha comes in and shuts the door. After Elijah prays and lies on the child, the child comes back to life. Hope, once again, was realized.

Questions for Day 11

1. How have you seen hope realized in your life?
2. The Shunammite didn't hesitate to run to Elisha for help. How influential do you believe Elisha had become in her life?
3. Do you think it is significant that the Shunammite laid her son down on Elisha's bed? Was she reminding God and Elisha of her kindness to him?
4. What is a situation in your life right now that you need to remain hopeful about? A lost friend or family member? A work situation? An addiction?

Prayer for Day 11

Father, remind me that you are a God in whom we can hope. We thank you for your promises of eternal life to all who cling to your Son. Help me to remain hopeful in situations that seem hopeless. Remind me that when things don't turn out the way I feel they should, you always do what's best.

DAY 12
FUTURE HOPE

She came and fell at his feet, bowing to the ground. Then she picked up her son and went out (2 Kings 4:37).

Do You Have a Future Hope?

America has been trending away from God for many years now. According to consistent Barna polling, those in America who identified as atheist, agnostic, or non-religious were 11 percent in 2003. Just 15 years later the same group had risen to 21 percent.[1] These are people that surround you all day. These are people who are born, grow up, live, get jobs, have families, and die without any hope of eternity. They live robotic lives without God and never realize their purpose of existence. If Christians are not open about their faith and sharing the gospel of Jesus Christ and the future hope that we have of eternal life (John 3:16), we are not keeping the second greatest command of "love your neighbor as yourself." We must be preachers of a future hope!

Before You Get Too Excited About Our Story

You must remember that the Shunammite's boy is not alive today. Even though he was raised from the dead, his resurrection was temporary. Daniel and I refer to this act of God as a resuscitation rather than a true resurrection. As you will see later in this book, by our definition there has only been one real resurrection. Interestingly enough, the story of the Shunammite ends quickly. She picks up her son from Elisha's room and "went out." That's it. Apparently, they go on to live a normal life, hopefully free of farming accidents. However long they lived after that, death still came to them. Because of that fact, we see that no matter the miracles we witness today, we still live in a world cursed by death. The story of the Shunammite's son is exciting in the moment that you read it but becomes a touch discouraging when you think about the fact that he dies again. The story leaves you realizing that God can raise the dead and wondering why God doesn't raise all of the dead. After all, if God has that kind of power, why doesn't he just use it instead of allowing our loved ones to pass on?

A Future Hope

Our highlighted story in this section leaves us yearning for resurrection. It makes us long to see our loved ones who have passed away come back to life. But not like the Shunammite's son. We want our families to come to life and never taste death again. The awesome thing is that this is exactly what God has planned for his people – but not yet.

The story of the Shunammite's son coming back to life shows us how things will be for God's people in the future. The Scriptures tell us that we have a future hope if we trust in Jesus. This hope is not one that means we will be raised and die again, but we will be like our Lord, raised, never to taste death again. Jesus wasn't merely resuscitated, he was resurrected, never to die again. 1 John 3:2 says, "Beloved, we are God's children now, and what we will be has not yet appeared; but we know that when he appears we shall be like him, because we shall see him as he is." This hope of being like him is reiterated in several passages as you will see fleshed out later in this book. This great story of the Shunammite's son hints early on to God's people that death can be overcome and swallowed up by the power of God.

Do You Have a Future Hope?
I want to finish today's devotion the same way I opened it – by asking the simple question of whether or not you have hope of a future resurrection. Do you believe that Jesus not only rolled away the stone that was placed on his tomb but will also one day resurrect all the saints in glory? Are you struggling with having faith in his promises? As our culture continues to slide toward atheism, agnosticism, and the non-religious, you must realize that these are people with no future hope. We are not people who live as if we have no hope. We believe that one day, we will all be resurrected to never die again!

"For this perishable body must put on the imperishable, and this mortal body must put on immortality. When the perishable puts on the imperishable, and the mortal puts on immortality, then shall come to pass the saying that is written: 'Death is swallowed up in victory.' 'O death, where is your victory? O death, where is your sting?' The sting of death is sin, and the power of sin is the law. But thanks be to God, who gives us the victory through our Lord Jesus Christ" (1 Corinthians 15:53-57).

Questions for Day 12

1. Do the statistics of the rise in atheism, agnosticism, and non-religion in our culture today surprise you?
2. What do you think is keeping so many people in America from trusting in Jesus today?
3. What is the difference between the resurrection of the Shunammite's son and the resurrection of Jesus?
4. What does 1 John say that our resurrected bodies will be like?

Prayer for Day 12

Lord, thank you for conquering death through a resurrection that is eternal. I also thank you that one day all who are found in Christ will be raised never to die again. Lord, I cry out to you for the lost and unbelieving in America. Please use me and your church to stir the world's affections for your beloved Son, Jesus.

Notes for Resurrection 2: Son of the Shunammite Woman

Day 9

[1] John Branch, January 9, 2015. https://www.nytimes.com/2015/01/10/sports/kevin-jorgeson-completes-crucial-pitch-on-el-capitans-dawn-wall.html.

[2] Ibid.

Day 12

[1] Barna Group: Tracking the Growth and Decline of Religious Segments: The Rise of Atheism https://www.barna.com/rise-of-atheism/.

Resurrection 3

2 Kings 13:20-21

DAY 13
THE POWER OF TOUCH

And as a man was being buried ... the man touched the bones of Elisha, he revived and stood on his feet (2 Kings 13:21).

The Need for Touch

According to popular psychology, a vast amount of research exists demonstrating humanity's tremendous need for touch. "Skin-to-skin contact in even the first hour after birth has been shown to help regulate newborns' temperature, heart rate, breathing and decreases crying."[1] Studies using PET scans have found that the brain quiets in response to stress when a person's hand is held.[2] God wired us to require and desire human contact.

A Whole New Level

In this historical account of Elisha, we see the power of human touch taken to a whole new level. Elisha had died and had been buried according to the custom of the ancient Israelites. On this day, some Israelites were burying another of their countrymen. During the burial processional, foreign marauders were seen coming across the border. This sight caused immediate panic. Those gathered for this funeral procession immediately became concerned for their own welfare and for the welfare of their families and homes. In their haste, those carrying the deceased quickly threw the body into the tomb where Elisha's body had been laid. The body of the deceased Israelite came into contact with the bones of Elisha. Immediately, the man was revived, stood, and most likely joined the other Israelites in fleeing from the marauders.

Demonstrating Love

As we prepare our hearts and minds for the celebration of Easter, remember that the motivation for Jesus to come and sacrifice himself on the cross and rise again from the grave was love: his love for the Father and his love for us. Additionally, Jesus teaches us that the greatest commandment is to "love the Lord your God" and the second is to "love your neighbor." Who has God placed in your life that needs to feel loved? Maybe it has been a while since you've given your teenager a hug and told them you loved them. Maybe your marriage has experienced a drought of affection. Maybe at church this week the Lord will show you someone who just needs a handshake or a pat on the back. These simple, non-threatening forms of physical touch go a long way.

Be intentional. Lead with love. Don't underestimate the power of touch.

Questions for Day 13

1. In what kind of home did you grow up? Was it affectionate, unaffectionate, or in between?
2. If you have trouble showing affection, why do you think that is?
3. If you have children, when was the last time you told them you loved them?
4. If you don't volunteer at your church, have you considered volunteering to be a greeter, where you can welcome people to the gathering with a fist bump, handshake, or pat on the back?

Prayer for Day 13

Lord, thank you that you love me. Thank you for those you have placed in my life who have demonstrated that love to me. As you continue to fill me with your Spirit, help me to demonstrate your love to others in tangible ways.

DAY 14
THE POWER OF FEAR

And as a man was being buried, behold, a marauding band was seen and the man was thrown into the grave of Elisha (2 Kings 13:21).

Irrational Fear

A few weeks ago, I (Daniel) took my eight-year-old daughter to the dentist for a routine check-up and a cleaning. This was her first visit to this dentist because our previous dentist refused to see her anymore. I could not understand why any dentist would refuse service to my sweet little eight-year-old. My wife insisted that I be the one to take Noel this time. I quickly agreed but had no idea what I was about to witness.

We arrived a few minutes early and checked in. They escorted us back to the X-ray machine to take some simple images of Noel's teeth. As Noel sat on the X-ray chair and they began to help her insert an oral piece for the X-ray, I witnessed an unbelievable and immediate change in the disposition of my daughter. Noel is a fun-loving, easy-going girl with quite a bit of spunk and personality. That girl immediately left the building and was replaced with a supernaturally strong, panicked, screaming purple minion (you need to see *Minions*). My jaw dropped. The shocked hygienist helplessly looked up at me as if I had the solution. I called my wife.

Fear's Response

It was a funeral. They were in the procession, carrying the body of one who had been their friend, family member, or coworker. They were grieving, reminiscing – wondering what life was going to look like without him. Suddenly, word came of marauders coming to attack and plunder the nearby towns and villages. In this instant, the grief and mourning were replaced by one of the most powerful emotions known to mankind – fear.

Isn't it amazing that in that instant these people appear to have forgotten their grief, their loss, and the importance of burying their friend and loved one? Fear can have the effect of causing us to lose all sense of reason. It is, indeed, a powerful emotion – when that sense of survival kicks in and we go into self-preservation mode, everything else seems to fade in our minds and affections.

Fear's Solution

All emotions, including fear, serve as warning indicators to us. When I have the emotion of anger, that is telling me something is going on in my heart. When I have the emotion of fear, that is telling me that perhaps I am in danger. So, how do we combat that fear when it becomes unhealthy?

1 John 4:18b tells us, "Perfect love casts out fear." The answer to overcoming fear is to remember the power of God, remember his faithfulness, and remember he loves you and is with you. When King David writes Psalm 23, he states, "Even though I walk through the valley of the shadow of death, I will fear no evil." And what is David's reasoning for not fearing evil? He goes on to say, "for you are with me; your rod and staff, they comfort me." David's solution to fear is to acknowledge that God is with him – just like he is with us.

Many have wondered why the Holy Spirit chose to include this very short account of a man encountering Elisha's bones and being raised to life. One answer we will suggest in tomorrow's devotion. But it is a great reminder of the power of fear and how all of us deal with it – or fail to deal with it. God doesn't want us to live in fear but in peace and communion with him. Let his perfect love cast out your fear today.

Questions for Day 14
1. What is a fear that tempts you to panic?
2. How can the reality of Jesus' presence with you lessen your fear?
3. Is there something right now that you are afraid of that you need to turn over to Jesus?
4. How would your life look different today if you were living with absolutely no fear?

Prayer for Day 14
Lord, thank you that you love me. I confess that I have some fear. Please give me courage and trust in you, and constantly remind me that you are with me. Lord, I turn my fears over to you, and I ask you for the peace that only you can give, in Jesus' name.

DAY 15
THE POWER OF GOD'S PROMISE

When they had crossed, Elijah said to Elisha, "Ask what I shall do for you, before I am taken from you." And Elisha said, "Please let there be a double portion of your spirit on me" (2 Kings 2:9).

What's the Connection?

As you've been reading this very short passage this week about this man whose corpse inadvertently touched the bones of Elisha and sprang to life, you've probably been wondering, "Why is this little story seemingly just randomly inserted here?" Truly, looking at the context, this insertion does nothing to enhance the previous writings, nor is it necessary to introduce the next historical episode. So why did the Holy Spirit, through the author, keep this brief, two-sentence insertion in the Scripture? Perhaps, it has to do with a promise.

A Promise Kept

As Elisha began his ministry, he attached himself to the prophet Elijah. Although Elijah had not sought out a protege, he allowed the persistent Elisha to accompany him in his final days. On the day the Lord was to take Elijah, Elisha was aware that Elijah's time was at hand to depart this world. He simply refused to leave the prophet's side.

In their last conversation, Elijah asks Elisha what he can do for his protégé. Elisha's response is profound and fascinating. He asks for a double portion of the prophet's spirit. Elijah responds with a normal prophetic response, "If you see me when I am taken, it will be so" (2 Kings 2:10). As the Lord would have it, Elisha was there and saw God take Elijah up to heaven in the chariot of fire. So Elisha knew that the Lord had granted his request, thus granting a double portion of Elijah's spirit.

Even Better

Examining the miracles performed by Elijah leaves one in awe of how God used this prophet in Old Testament times. Elijah performed 14 miracles before he was caught up to heaven in a whirlwind riding the chariot of fire. How would Elisha top this? What would a double portion of Elijah's spirit look like?

As we read 2 Kings, we see that Elisha essentially did the same types of miracles that Elijah had performed, only better – and more of them. In fact, interestingly, at the time of Elisha's death, he had performed 27 miracles. Now any decent math student will quickly catch that Elijah had performed 14 and Elisha 27. Elisha was one miracle shy of truly doubling Elijah's number of miracles.

Maybe God was off by one? Maybe one of Elisha's miracles was not recorded? Or can we just round up to make the numbers work out? The answer to all these questions is a resounding "NO." God doesn't make mistakes. God is never off by one. His promises are precise, clear, and assured.

The 28th Miracle
Even the death of Elisha was not able to prevent God from accomplishing his promise to grant Elisha that double portion of Elijah's spirit. As the Jewish men quickly put the body of their countryman into the tomb of Elisha and the bodies touched, God kept his word. He fulfilled his promise by energizing that body through the bones of his servant Elisha's corpse. The 28th miracle was complete. God kept his word! He is the promise-keeping God.

God hasn't changed. He still keeps his promises. He has both the power and the authority to make the promise and to see that it comes about. He will always keep his promises to you. Hebrews 6:18 says, "it is impossible for God to lie." Trust him. Not even death can stop God from keeping his promises.

Questions for Day 15
1. What is one promise God has made to you through his word that you are banking on?
2. Why is it impossible for God to lie?
3. If death can't stop God from keeping his promise, what is a situation in which you now feel more confident that God is going to keep his promise to you?

Prayer for Day 15
Lord, thank you that you have the power to keep all of your promises. Increase my faith and trust in you, knowing that if you've said it, you will deliver. When I begin to doubt or question if you'll keep your promises, remind me of your power and commitment to your word.

Miracles in the Career of Elijah
1. Causing the rain to cease for three and a half years - 1 Kings 17:1
2. Being fed by the ravens - 1 Kings 17:4
3. The jar of meal and jug of oil - 1 Kings 17:14
4. Resurrection of the widow's son - 1 Kings 17:22
5. Calling of fire from heaven on the altar - 1 Kings 18:38
6. Causing it to rain - 1 Kings 18:45
7. Prophecy that Ahab's sons would all be destroyed - 1 Kings 21:22
8. Prophecy that Jezebel would be eaten by dogs - 1 Kings 21:23
9. Prophecy that Ahaziah would die of his illness - 2 Kings 1:4
10. Calling fire from heaven upon the first 50 soldiers - 2 Kings 1:10
11. Calling fire from heaven upon the second 50 soldiers - 2 Kings 1:12
12. Parting of the Jordan - 2 Kings 2:8
13. Prophecy that Elisha should have a double portion of his spirit - 2 Kings 2:10
14. Being caught up to heaven in a whirlwind - 2 Kings 2:11

Miracles in the Career of Elisha
1. Parting of the Jordan - 2 Kings 2:14
2. Healing of the waters - 2 Kings 2:21
3. Curse of the she bears - 2 Kings 2:24
4. Filling of the valley with water - 2 Kings 3:17
5. Deception of the Moabites with the valley of blood - 2 Kings 3:22
6. The vessels of oil - 2 Kings 4:4
7. Prophecy that the Shunammite woman would have a son - 2 Kings 4:16
8. Resurrection of the Shunammite's son - 2 Kings 4:34
9. Healing of the gourds - 2 Kings 4:41
10. The bread - 2 Kings 4:43
11. Healing of Naaman - 2 Kings 5:14
12. Perception of Gehazi's transgression - 2 Kings 5:26
13. Cursing Gehazi with leprosy - 2 Kings 5:27
14. Floating of the axe head - 2 Kings 6:6
15. Prophecy of the Syrian battle plans - 2 Kings 6:9
16. Vision of the chariots - 2 Kings 6:17
17. Smiting the Syrian army with blindness - 2 Kings 6:18
18. Restoring the sight of the Syrian army - 2 Kings 6:20
19. Prophecy of the end of the great famine - 2 Kings 7:1
20. Prophecy that the scoffing nobleman would see, but not partake of, the abundance - 2 Kings 7:2
21. Deception of the Syrians with the sound of chariots - 2 Kings 7:6
22. Prophecy of the seven-year famine - 2 Kings 8:1
23. Prophecy of Benhadad's untimely death - 2 Kings 8:10
24. Prophecy of Hazael's cruelty to Israel - 2 Kings 8:12
25. Prophecy that Jehu would smite the house of Ahab - 2 Kings 9:7
26. Prophecy that Joash would smite the Syrians at Aphek - 2 Kings 13:17
27. Prophecy that Joash would smite Syria thrice but not consume it - 2 Kings 13:19
28. Resurrection of the man touched by his bones - 2 Kings 13:21

DAY 16
THE POWER OF HOPE

... as soon as the man touched the bones of Elisha, he revived and stood on his feet (2 Kings 13:21b).

Hope that Inspires

When I (Daniel) was six years old, my family and I had just moved into a new neighborhood. We had bought a house on a cul-de-sac where other families with kids lived and played. About that time, my older brother decided it was time for me to learn how to ride a bicycle. The only problem was that my confidence in my ability to learn did not match the confidence that my brother had in me. I fought it. I was just fine with my training wheels. After several days of back-and-forth arguing, I happened to see our next-door neighbor's daughter on the cul-de-sac riding her bike – and she was only five! This was what I needed to see. If she could do it, so could I.

Other peoples' stories of hope and inspiration can fuel us to persevere in difficult times. In 1836, the Battle of the Alamo inspired Texans to rally and defeat the Mexican armies at San Jacinto. The story of Corrie Ten Boom's faith and perseverance in surviving life in a Nazi concentration camp has inspired many in their quest to persevere in trying times. Even smaller stories like the next-door neighbor riding her bike inspired me to have the courage and concern to give bike riding a shot. Hope has the power to move us in a direction we didn't think we could go.

Tough Times

In 2 Kings 13 the Jewish people are under heavy oppression at the hand of the Syrians (22). They had very few freedoms and lived in fear. Would they ever be rid of this oppressive King Hazael and the Syrian soldiers? Constant oppression takes a toll on a people's psyche, morale, and outlook. Life can become seemingly pointless and futile. Hope is all but squelched.

The Lord's Steadfast Love

Psalm 18:50 says that the Lord "shows steadfast love to his anointed, to David and his offspring forever." The descendants of David had suffered for years under Syria's oppression. But then – seemingly randomly – this dead Jewish man touched Elisha's bones and came back to life. No doubt, news of this traveled near and far. God's power was still at work. Even the dead man of God was still having an effect. God wasn't silent. God had not abandoned them. Miracles still were happening. Perhaps, just perhaps, there was still hope that they would be delivered from these Syrians.

Shortly after this resurrection event, King Joash of Israel defeated the Syrians and recovered the cities of Israel (vs. 25). The hope inspired by this third resurrection was realized as God once again delivered his people from oppression.

What kinds of oppression do you find yourself under? Perhaps your financial woes are oppressive? Your physical health? Maybe you have a relationship that is oppressive? Do you feel a heavy weight on your shoulders because your marriage isn't what you want it to be or what it should be? Take hope in the resurrection! God is still on his throne. God's power is still at work! God is still changing hearts and minds all over this world! His steadfast love is with you.

Questions for Day 16
1. If you heard that God had brought someone you know back to life, how would that impact your outlook on your problems?
2. Is there anything oppressive in your life? If so, what is it?
3. If you think you've lost hope, why – according to this story and the resurrection of Jesus – should you never truly lose all hope?

Prayer for Day 16
Lord, rekindle hope in my heart and mind. Make my hope be in you and help this hope to only grow and grow – whatever my circumstances. Lord, since you've conquered death, you can conquer anything. Take my hurt, my oppression, and my despair. Transform me into a person filled with hope, joy, and love.

… as the man touched the bones of Elisha… (2 Kings 13:21).

The Race for Relics

Early in church history, churches would collect and seek out the bones of the martyrs and other physical items of Christian significance. This practice quickly grew and became a source of superstition and competition in the early and medieval church. Sacred relics seemed to indicate God's special favor on a particular church. Thus, great pursuits ensued. And, as expected, many false claims abounded. In fact, so many churches claimed to have pieces of Christ's actual cross that, in the words of Augustine quoted by John Calvin:

> *There is no abbey so poor as not to have a specimen [of the cross]. In some places there are large fragments, as at the Holy Chapel in Paris, at Poitiers, and at Rome, where a good-sized crucifix is said to have been made of it. In brief, if all the pieces that could be found were collected together, they would make a big ship-load. Yet the Gospel testifies that a single man was able to carry it.*[3]

Even today, many devout Catholics are encouraged to kiss and touch these relics in the hope that through them and the intercession of the saint (to whom the relics belonged) God would grant grace, a healing, or even a miracle.[4]

No Relics Necessary

Many who still maintain that there is power in relics refer to this story of Elisha's bones as biblical evidence. However, unlike today's approach to relics, these pallbearers weren't seeking a miracle. They didn't have any special prayer service. In fact, they even seem a little oblivious as to whose tomb they threw their deceased comrade into due to their panicked state.

The New Testament makes very clear that we don't receive grace through mere relics or physical objects or even religious actions. The apostle Paul is very clear when he says, "For by grace you have been saved through faith. And this is not of your own doing; it is the gift of God, not a result of works, so that no one may boast" (Ephesians 2:8-9).

We don't receive grace through sacred bones or splinters of Jesus' cross. We receive grace through faith alone. Are you seeking to receive

God's grace through efforts on your part? Maybe through an old family Bible you've held onto but not really read? Maybe you're hoping you're just good enough to get in on that grace of God? I've got bad news for you – it doesn't work that way. No physical item is good enough to give us grace. And none of us is good enough to earn God's grace.

But the good news – Jesus is good enough. He satisfied the "good" requirement – and he is the only one who could because he is God. Yet, he sacrificed himself on the cross in our place so we could receive from him the gift of his goodness credited to our lives, and he took our sin and guilt from us. The apostle Paul says it like this: "For our sake [God] made [Jesus] to be sin who knew no sin, so that in him we might become the righteousness of God" (2 Corinthians 5:21).

What a trade! This is the gospel. This is Jesus and his love for you. This is grace!

Questions for Day 17
1. Have you ever been superstitious about anything? What?
2. When it comes to whether God should allow you into his kingdom, in what or whom are you trusting for that answer?
3. Have you ever trusted in Jesus as the solution to your need for forgiveness and salvation and committed to following him?

Prayer for Day 17
Lord Jesus, your grace is enough. I don't need any superstitious items. I don't need just so many good works. I don't just need religious actions. I need you. Thank you that what you did is enough. Thank you that you died in my place, rose again, and give forgiveness to me.

DAY 18
THE POWER OF LEGACY

… thrown into the grave of Elisha… (2 Kings 13:21).

A Family Legacy

I (Daniel) will never forget as a ten-year-old, going to our big family reunion on my mom's side. My mom and dad both grew up in Sevier County, Tennessee, in the Smoky Mountains. This particular family reunion was at my grandparents' place. They owned and operated an apple orchard in their retirement — a beautiful scene for a family reunion. Once all had arrived and the food had been set out, my grandfather asked the Lord's blessing. Upon "amen" all the sounds of family filled the air. Food being eaten, soda cans popping open, kids shouting and shrieking as they ran and played, parents correcting and scolding over bad manners or rough play. I noticed in the midst of all the frolicking that my grandfather (I called him Big Daddy) had withdrawn to his favorite bench swing in his yard. Sitting by himself he possessed a contemplative expression as he observed his family. This family was quite large. My grandparents had five children, all of whom had their own spouses, children, and even grandchildren. Yes, there was quite a crowd present for this family reunion.

As I finished off a ham sandwich and sipped on my soda, I decided to go plop down on the swing next to Big Daddy. He welcomed the company. I asked him, "Whatcha doin,' Big Daddy?" I will never forget his response. He said, "Well, Daniel, I am thanking the good Lord for this family one by one. Every member of this family has trusted in Jesus, even the great-grandchildren old enough." Big Daddy was smiling and had moist eyes. He had no greater joy than to know that his family loved Jesus. He was leaving a legacy of faith.

Beyond a Lifetime

As I sit here at my desk writing this, I'm looking at some books I always keep nearby. Books written by Charles H. Spurgeon, Jonathan Edwards, and Richard Baxter. All three of these men lived centuries ago. All of them were mighty men of God in their day leading their churches and even their countries in great spiritual revivals and awakenings. Yet, these three men also directly impact me. They mentor me. They challenge me. They rebuke and encourage me. Their work continues beyond their lifetimes.

Elisha's work continued beyond his lifetime. He had lived his life in total, surrendered allegiance to the Lord. He had challenged kings, guided kings, anointed kings. He had faithfully represented the Lord to the nation of Israel. He had impacted many lives. Yet, his work continued even after his death.

What kind of legacy are you leaving? If your epitaph were to be written today, what would it say? How would your family and coworkers remember you? What kinds of stories would be told? Are you living a life that will have an impact beyond your death?

Questions for Day 18

1. Whose life is still impacting you even though that person is no longer living? How are they continuing to impact you?
2. Who is one person you've really invested in and made a difference in their life?
3. Who is someone that you haven't invested in yet but that you sense the Lord leading you or already using you to have a kingdom impact upon?

Prayer for Day 18

Lord, I know you created me to make a difference. I want to leave a legacy of faith in you, Jesus. Grow me and use me to make disciples, to mentor and encourage others in their faith journey with you.

Notes for Resurrection 3: The Israelite Man

Day 13

[1] Ferber, Feldman & Makhoul (2010), "The development of maternal touch across the first year of life," *Early Human Development*, Volume 84, Issue 6.
[2] Field, T. (2010)," Touch for socioemotional and physical well-being: A review" *Developmental Review*, Volume 30, Issue 4, Pages 367-383.

Day 17

[3] Augustine, 'On the Labour of Monks', quoted by John Calvin, *Inventory of Relics* (Still Waters Revival Books, Puritan Hard Drive, 2009), Page 302.
[4] www.banneroftruth.org/us/resources/articles/2015/the-veneration-of-relics/#note-3.

Resurrection 4

SON OF THE WIDOW FROM NAIN

Luke 7:11-17

DAY 19
COMPASSION: HE SEES

And when the Lord saw her, he had compassion on her (Luke 7:13).

I Can't See You...

It was super weird. Maybe you've been there before. I (Martin) was in the grocery store and saw someone I knew out of the corner of my eye. As I looked over, they quickly moved their head the other direction and took off around the corner, acting as if they didn't see me. *Hmmmm*, I thought to myself. *Maybe they didn't see me.* So, I pursued. As I rounded the corner and looked down the aisle they had entered, they were hightailing it away. It was obvious that they didn't want to talk to me or acknowledge me. This weird encounter made me do a little soul searching. Do I talk too much? Do they really not like me? What in the world just happened? It feels downright strange for someone who knows you to ignore you and act like they never saw you.

All Powerful. All Seeing.

When we read about Jesus in the New Testament, we realize quickly in the Gospels that he is God in human form. John 1:3 says, "All things were made through him, and without him was not any thing made that was made." Colossians 1:16 goes even further into detail when it says, "For by him all things were created, in heaven and on earth, visible and invisible, whether thrones or dominions or rulers or authorities – all things were created through him and for him." He (Jesus) made everything! Not only did he make everything, but he is also interested in the details of everything he made. Hebrews 1:3 says, "He upholds the universe by the word of his power." Nothing escapes him, and no detail is too small for him to notice. As theologian R.C. Sproul tweeted in 2017, "There is not one piece of cosmic dust that is outside the scope of God's sovereign providence."[1] This should give us assurance as God's people that he knows our difficulties and pain, and he acts in a way that is always best for us, even if we don't understand it. His eternal purposes are often hidden from us, but we are never ignored. He always sees us and never ignores us!

The Lord Sees the Widow

Jesus didn't see the widow from Nain and walk the other direction, pretending to not see her distress. When Jesus saw the pain that this mother was enduring (the loss of her only son), he immediately chose to become involved. The King of the entire universe was taking note of the visible distress this unnamed widow was going through in this virtually unknown town. If anyone had the excuse of a busy schedule or too many things to do, it was Jesus. He could have simply seen the casket pass by, felt sorry for the lady, and then kept walking to his next appointment. But compassion sees.

Do You See?

Have you ever seen a video of someone walking with their face pointed down at their phone, and then they fall into a fountain? If not, there are a plethora of videos out there where you can see people with their heads down looking at their screens while walking into fountains, glass doors, or other things. For those involved in the accidents, it is a wake-up call to look around them. If your schedule, your phone, or your hobbies keep you from seeing the needs of others in front of you, it may be time for you to begin looking outside of yourself again. It is so easy to become self-consumed, isn't it? This story in the Gospel demonstrates to us that our Lord walked with his head up, looking to spread his compassion to the world. It is impossible to have compassion on people who need it if you don't see them.

Since 2010, I (Martin) have been involved with numerous churches in several different states, trying to bring awareness to the great physical and spiritual poverty in many communities in rural Zambia, Africa. It has been amazing through the years to see people step away from their jobs, their busy schedules, and often cell service, and into a poor African village to see the lost and hungry for the first time. I have witnessed the life-changing impact of these trips for so many, simply because they took the time to see. Because Jesus saw this woman in her desperation, he had compassion. There are people around you today that need that same compassion. Jesus sees. Do you?

Questions for Day 19

1. Have you ever had someone pretend like they didn't see you? How did that make you feel? Be honest. Have you ever done that to someone else?
2. Is it shocking to think that Jesus is the God of the universe and still takes time to have compassion for the needs of his people? How does that make you feel?
3. Is your schedule too cluttered to have compassion on the needy around you? How are you seeing like Jesus?
4. What needs to change in your life for you to better see the needs of others?

Prayer for Day 19

Lord, I thank you that you are sovereign over the universe. You control every molecule and still have time for me. I thank you that you are not blind to the needs of your people but care and always do what's right for them in every situation. Help me today, Lord, to see the needs of those around me, to have compassion, and to get involved.

DAY 20
COMPASSION: HE FEELS

And when the Lord saw her, he had compassion on her (Luke 7:13).

Jesus *Feels* Compassion

Is an orphanage a good thing? You might be thinking, "What kind of a question is that? Of course an orphanage is a good thing!" But think about it. An orphanage only exists because children have no parents to care for them. An orphanage may be "good," but an orphanage is not ideal. The problem is that we don't live in an ideal world, do we? We live in a world stained with sin, death, and despair. An orphanage is a way of lessening the sting and pain of the effects of being without parents. Compassion is the same way. In an ideal world, there would be no need for compassion. But since we live in a broken world with broken people, compassion for others is very necessary. Likely, compassion is one of the emotions that led to someone starting an orphanage. A very basic definition of the English word "compassion" is: "sympathetic pity and concern for the sufferings or misfortunes of others."[2]

The Greek word for compassion in our text comes from the word *splangnon*. While the basic meaning of the word is the same, the Greek has the idea that the feeling of compassion begins in the "inner body parts."[3] Have you ever been so sad about something that it made you sick to your stomach? This is the root meaning of the Greek word for compassion. When Jesus saw this widow who had lost her son, he had a physical reaction to the pain and grief that the woman was feeling over her loss. He *felt* compassion for her over the loss of her son.

The Orphan and the Widow

I (Martin) have had the opportunity to visit several orphanages through the years. In fact, two of my children are adopted. One of my sons is from Siberia and the other is from Ethiopia. Every time that I have walked inside an orphanage, I experience that physical emotion of the Greek word for compassion. I want to help! I want to defend and care for the orphans. I feel a physical response to my compassion for the children who need forever homes. Have you felt this emotion yourself in the past?

In our Bible story, this man who had died was a "single orphan" before his death – meaning his father had already passed away. No doubt he was caring for his mother before his untimely death. We know from the Scriptures that God has a special heart for both orphans and widows. We can see, therefore, that this event would have especially touched the heart of Christ.

Isaiah 1:17 says, "Learn to do good; seek justice, correct oppression; bring justice to the fatherless, plead the widow's cause." James 1:27 says, "Religion that is pure and undefiled before God the Father is this: to visit orphans and widows in their affliction, and to keep oneself unstained from the world." When Jesus saw this poor, grieving widow and her dead orphan son, his guts were stirred to help them. His heart broke for her pain, and he sprang to action. Jesus' compassion for this woman and her son wasn't something that merely stirred up his emotions. His feelings led him to do something for this woman in her time of pain and desperation.

Don't Stew. Do.
Colossians 3:12a says, "Put on then, as God's chosen ones, holy and beloved, compassionate hearts." The brokenness that we see around us often hardens us to the pain of others. It can also frustrate us, leading to indifference or cynicism. Compassionate hearts should be something we regularly practice not only amongst other Christians but also to a lost and dying world. Instead of being moved to anger over sin, death, and destruction, put on a compassionate heart like our Lord Jesus Christ. Feel the pain of others, and then do something about it!

Questions for Day 20
1. What makes the Greek word for compassion unique?
2. Have you ever felt biblical compassion over someone's situation? Enough that your guts hurt? If so, share it with others.
3. Why do you think that the Lord's heart is especially stirred over widows and orphans? Is yours?
4. Why is it so easy for us to become frustrated at the brokenness in the world? What kind of hearts should we put on when we see brokenness? Hint: Colossians 3:12a.

Prayer for Day 20
Father, I thank you that you have a heart for the most vulnerable in society. Help me to be an advocate for the poor, needy, widows, and orphans. I pray that you would give me a heart of compassion like Jesus. Give me a heart that truly feels the pain of others. I pray, then, that you would give me the resolve to step in and be as helpful as I can with the gospel always on my lips.

DAY 21
COMPASSION: HE SPEAKS

"Do not weep.… Young man, I say to you, arise" (Luke 7:13b; 14b).

Powerful Voices
Some people have astonishing voices, don't they? Liam Neeson's voice as Aslan in *The Chronicles of Narnia* is unforgettable. What Southern Baptist hasn't gotten chills from the powerful preaching voice of Adrian Rodgers. How about James Earl Jones' famous and quite intimidating voice as Darth Vader? I remember learning in seminary years ago about the preaching of George Whitefield during the First Great Awakening in America. He was said to have a voice like "the roar of a lion."[4] In fact, Whitefield's voice was so impressive that Ben Franklin decided to do an experiment when Whitefield arrived in Philadelphia in 1739. Franklin determined through his experiment that more than 30,000 people could hear Whitefield preach at one time![5] When one keeps in mind that this is before the age of modern amplification, the feat becomes even more impressive.

Although we have no record as to the sound or loudness of Jesus' voice, I believe history makes it clear that no one had a more powerful voice than Jesus Christ, God's Son. Think of Jesus' words to calm the storm, simply saying, "Peace, be still" – and a horrible tempest is at once soothed (Mark 4:39). Or how about the words, "Get up, take up your bed, and walk," to a man who hadn't walked in 38 years! Hebrews 1:3 takes the power of Jesus to an even higher level when it says, "He [Jesus] is the radiance of the glory of God and the exact imprint of his nature, and he upholds the universe by the word of his power." I don't think that anyone's words compare to the words of Jesus. In fact, he (Jesus) is called "the Word of God made flesh" (John 1:1,14).

A Word for the Widow and a Word for the Orphan
As we turn our attention back to the story of Jesus bringing this orphan back to life in Luke 7, we see similarities with another famous story from the Gospel of John that I want to point out to you. Can you guess which story I'm referencing? It's the story of Jesus raising Lazarus from the dead (John 11). In the story of Lazarus, we see a key verb being used in John 11:38 regarding Jesus. It is the verb *embrimaomai*. This verb is sometimes translated "deeply moved."

However, in "classical Greek this word is used of horses 'snorting' as they prepare to charge the enemy in battle. In the Greek Old Testament, the term refers to 'indignation' (Lamentations 2:6) and rage

(Daniel 11:30)."[6] In other words, Jesus is mad at death! New Testament professor Scott Duvall says of this verse, "As Jesus goes to the tomb of Lazarus, he isn't just overwhelmed with sadness and grief. He's also righteous with rage. He's fighting mad. He's angry at sin, suffering, disease, and most of all, death!"[7] I don't believe it is a stretch to think that Jesus was angry at death in our Luke 7 passage. Jesus says to this widow, "Do not weep." He follows this with, "Young man, I say to you, arise!" These two powerful statements by Jesus are both life-changing and life-giving to this poor woman and her son.

The Voice of Jesus

We may not be able to hear the voice of Jesus today, but we can certainly read the words of Jesus he has left us in the holy Scriptures. The Scriptures tell us that Jesus hates death, is fighting mad about it (John 11:38), and plans to cast it into the lake of fire on the last day (Revelation 20:14). Death is the final enemy to be permanently destroyed (1 Corinthians 15:26). When it is finally destroyed, we will hear his voice call us from on high. Jesus said, "Do not marvel at this, for an hour is coming when all who are in the tombs will hear his voice and come out, those who have done good to the resurrection of life, and those who have done evil to the resurrection of judgment" (John 5:28-29). This resurrection will be permanent. The widow's son was raised but died again. In the future, our resurrection will be like that of Jesus. We will all be raised, never to die again. When you think of those special people in your life whom you have lost to death, remind yourself of this: if they are found in Christ, you have a deliverer who is angered by death, will destroy it on the last day, and will call for their final resurrection. All it will take is the voice of Jesus.

Questions for Day 21

1. Who has a great voice that comes to your mind?
2. What famous man in history tried to measure how far George Whitefield's voice could travel?
3. Who has the most powerful voice in the universe? Can you prove your case from the Bible?
4. Instead of Jesus being "deeply moved" by death, what is a better translation of that word?
5. What will happen to death in the future? What will happen to believers and their loved ones who have already passed on?

Prayer for Day 21

Thank you, Jesus, for hating death! I thank you today for the promise that one day you will utterly destroy death and its effects on this earth. I thank you that you demonstrated your compassion and love to this poor orphan by raising him from the dead. I also thank you that you conquered death in your own body, permanently destroying the effects of sin and death.

DAY 22
COMPASSION: HE TOUCHES

Then he came up and touched the bier, and the bearers stood still (Luke 7:14a).

Touch – A Double-Edged Sword

As I (Martin) am writing this, Olympic gymnast Simone Biles won the bronze medal in balance beam less than 24 hours ago. However, the week leading up to this event had been very difficult for Biles and her family. Her aunt suddenly passed away, and Simone was dealing with a severe case of the "twisties" (second-guessing her instincts while in the air, which can lead to a potentially devastating injury). Biles will go down in history as one of the greats for her past achievements as well as for overcoming these things to win the bronze. However, Biles also explained that something else was bothering her that week as well. In a recent post, she talked about dealing with pain from the inappropriate touches she received while under the care of Larry Nassar. This man, a convicted serial molester, was sentenced to 175 years behind bars for the molestation of multiple Olympic gymnasts through the years. These touches, though years earlier, still affect Simone with deep emotional pain and guilty feelings.[8]

Touch can be bad, but touch can also be good. Touch can be a very powerful agent of love, confirmation, and kindness. No one had a more powerful, kind, healing touch than Jesus. Many times in the New Testament we see Jesus heal with the power of touch (Matthew 5:35-43; 8:1-4; 9:23-26). Jesus didn't have to touch these individuals to heal them, but he chose to do so. All Christ would have to do is say the word, and a person would be healed. But, in some cases, Jesus chose to touch others. I think the touch of Jesus would never be forgotten by the one who experienced it. Christ was so powerful that even when others touched him, they were healed. Consider the story of the woman who merely touched the fringe of Jesus' garment (Luke 8:44) and was instantly healed!

Jesus Touched the Hurting

Lepers were outcasts in the ancient world. They weren't allowed to get close to "normal" people with their skin diseases. Many of these poor souls were cast outside the camp into leper colonies to survive on their own. In fact, lepers had to yell that they were near when others accidently approached them. Leviticus 13:45 says, "The leprous person who has the disease shall wear torn clothes and let the hair of his head hang loose, and he shall cover his upper lip and cry out, 'Unclean, unclean.' "

Jesus changed all of that. Instead of becoming unclean by the touch of the leper, the leper became clean by the touch of Jesus. Jesus' touch was healing to those who experienced it, and it changed their lives. Consider Jesus' touch of the leper in Matthew 8:3, "And Jesus stretched out his hand and touched him, saying, 'I will; be clean.' And immediately his leprosy was cleansed."

The Bier (Coffin)
In Luke 7:14, Jesus touches the coffin and the man in it receives his life back. Can you imagine the joy that this poor mother felt as she saw her son receive his life back? This incredible story shows that the touch of Jesus is the most powerful touch the universe has ever seen.

Have you been touched by Jesus? I know I have. Ephesians 2:1 says that I was "dead in my trespasses and sins." Notice, the key word "dead." Just like in our passage, the dead can do nothing for themselves. Jesus must do something to bring the dead back to life. It also goes on to say that in verses 4-5, "But God, being rich in mercy, because of the great love with which he loved us, even when we were dead in our trespasses, made us alive together with Christ – by grace you have been saved." A spiritual resurrection has happened in your life if you have been born again. I remember the moment that Jesus touched me, and I became born again. Do you? If you haven't been born again, turn to Christ and he will raise you from spiritual death. There is a famous old hymn that is one of my favorites. It's called, "He Touched Me." This is the first verse. I hope that you have experienced the spiritual resurrection that it talks about.

> Shackled by a heavy burden
> 'Neath a load of guilt and shame
> Then the hand of Jesus touched me
> And now I am no longer the same
> He touched me, oh, He touched me
> And oh, the joy that floods my soul
> Something happened and now I know
> He touched me and made me whole.[9]

Questions for Day 22
1. Why do you think that Jesus chose to touch people sometimes when he healed them?
2. Can you remember an instance when Jesus chose to touch someone to heal them?
3. Why was it especially amazing when Jesus chose to touch a leper?
4. Did you notice in our story that Jesus didn't actually touch the man? What did he choose to touch to complete this miracle?

5. Have you been touched by Jesus and given eternal life? If so, how do you know?

Prayer for Day 22

Father, I thank you that you showed us that touch can be used for good. Thank you for your power and love for us. I thank you that you have the power to touch humans even now from heaven and give them new life. Thank you for eternal life through Jesus Christ!

DAY 23
COMPASSION: HE GIVES

And the dead man sat up and began to speak, and Jesus gave him to his mother (Luke 7:15).

Gifts

I (Martin) bet that you've received some great gifts during your lifetime. Think about it a minute. What was a gift that you received that just blew you away? A car when you turned 16? Maybe an unexpected trip to Hawaii funded by family members? Maybe it was a new gaming system or an airsoft gun. What gift was given to you that was special? Share it with those in the room if others are doing this devotional with you. Do you remember the feelings that you had toward those who gave you the gift? Did you feel endearment, love, and excitement toward them and their relationship with you?

In the early spring of 2006, Joanne Gadt walked into my office at First Baptist Church in little Lexington, Missouri, and told me that she had a surprise for me. Joanne was one of the senior adults in the church, and to make the announcement with her were several other seniors from her Sunday school class. I was honestly baffled. I had no idea what she was talking about or what they could be up to. As I sat there in my chair, my office filled with many seniors from the church; I felt totally caught off guard and a little worried. Then she said it: "Martin, we are so excited that in a couple of months you are graduating from seminary. We are thankful for the ministry that you have here at the church, and the senior adult ministry has bought you an all-expenses-paid trip to the Holy Land for your graduation!" I was shocked, amazed, disbelieving, and very grateful all at once. This kindness was completely unexpected and completely appreciated. By the way, the trip was amazing!

He Gives Life

Life is a gift, isn't it? Many times we see those in poverty in other parts of the world, and we feel sad for them. Our heart goes out to these people with thoughts of compassion, and it should. However, some of the happiest, most fulfilled people I have met in the world live in impoverished conditions. Have you ever heard the saying, "It's the little things in life"? This little saying attempts to reorient your thinking from what you don't have and redirect it to be grateful for the things you do have. Right now, you live in the "present." It is called the present because that is exactly what it is. It is a present from God to you. What are you going to do with it? Life moves quickly and now is the time to use your "present" for him.

A Grieving Mother No More

Jesus' power of resurrecting this dead man and giving him to his mother is a demonstration that he can do anything. In this moment of incredible grief for this mother, Jesus stretches out his hand, brings this man back to life, and gives him as a gift to his mother. Jesus "gave him to his mother." All of life is a gift from God. Since Jesus is the Creator of us all, this is the second time that God has given the gift of a son to this woman. When he was created at conception, it was Jesus who gave this man his life and now again as an adult. There are many mothers who have lost their children prematurely to death. The power of Jesus to raise this man demonstrates his clear power over death. In the end, all those who have died in Christ will be raised back to life. If you have lost a child to death and if they were clinging to Jesus, remember that soon you will be a grieving mother no more. Don't you know that after Jesus raised this man from the dead and gave him to his mother, there was incredible rejoicing in the family? No more would they get upset over silly things. No more would they fuss with each other. Because death had visited this mother and child once, you know that they now would appreciate their relationship more than ever. The sting of death can visit us at any moment. Are you making the most of the relationships with which God has gifted you?

Questions for Day 23

1. Think back to a special gift that you received in the past. What was it?
2. When you received gifts from others in the past, how did that make you feel toward them?
3. What "little things in life" bring you happiness and joy?
4. How could Jesus raising this dead man be the second time that he had given this man to his mother?
5. Are you thankful for the gift of life that God has given you?

Prayer for Day 23

God, thank you for how you have so wonderfully made me. I thank you for the gift of life and for the new life in Christ that you freely offer. I ask you to remind me each day of what you have given me and help me be grateful for it. Thank you, Jesus, for all the little things.

DAY 24
COMPASSION: GOD IS GLORIFIED

Fear seized them all, and they glorified God, saying, "A great prophet has arisen among us!" and "God has visited his people!" And this report about him spread through the whole of Judea and all the surrounding country (Luke 7:16-17).

They Glorified God

Notice that this great compassion that Jesus demonstrated toward this man and his mother spread everywhere. Obviously, the fact that the man was raised from the dead was the main reason for news spreading quickly, but undoubtedly, the care and compassion of Jesus were a big part of the news spreading as well. This act of Jesus was so amazing that the people glorified God because of it. The compassion of Jesus leads to the glory of God.

Have You Had the Chance to Show Compassion?

Have you ever been able to show someone the compassion of Jesus even though that person didn't deserve it? A few years ago, when I (Martin) was in Zambia, Africa, a young father (let's call him Danny) tried to steal some land from me. Danny had three kids kicking around in the dirt behind him when I went to meet him. He claimed that part of the property on which I was planning to build a school for the children of the community was on his land, and he wanted $2,000 for a small, square portion of the land. I knew that he was trying to take advantage of me and get me to pay him. I felt caught in a real conundrum. I knew that if I paid him money for this property, others would come and claim portions of it as well, trying to get more money out of me. If this happened, I might not ever get to finish the project. I told him that I wasn't going to pay it, but I needed some time to think. I was mad at Danny but knew that I needed to show him compassion.

That night, some friends and I prayed about this situation. I needed that property, and I needed the hearts of the people in the community. What to do? Then, God gave me the idea. I went back to Danny and told him that if he would sign a document saying that the land belonged to me, I would find American sponsors for his children to feed them every day and give them an education. Danny's friend, standing next to him, said, "Danny, you are crazy if you don't take this deal!" Danny agreed to the deal. He signed the paper. When I brought back the story to America, instantly people were ready to sponsor Danny's children. Now, all of Danny's children are growing up in Bethlehem Christian Academy. They are exposed to the gospel and to a church planted in that community despite the fact that Danny's dad was the village witch! Oh, and one really cool fact – Danny's niece recently came to faith in the gospel.

The News Spreads

"And this report about him spread through the whole of Judea and all the surrounding country." When we make compassion a priority, news of this compassion spreads, and God gets the glory. This simple act of compassion toward Danny's kids gave us good rapport in the community. Through the years as I've shared the story about Danny (along with other stories), I've watched God's people continue to get involved in real ways to make his glory known. Compassion is contagious. When we stay in God's word, we are consistently challenged – especially by the ministry of Jesus – to be compassionate toward others. When we are compassionate, God visits his people, the news spreads, and God is glorified.

Questions for Day 24

1. When was a time that you had to show compassion to someone who didn't deserve it?
2. When Jesus brought this man to life, what was the people's response?
3. What would you have done in the Danny situation? Do you think it was handled the right way, or would you have taken a different direction?
4. When someone shows compassion, the story spreads. When have you heard of compassion that someone showed toward someone else?
5. If you recalled a situation where someone showed compassion, how was God glorified in that situation?

Prayer for Day 24

Father, thank you that you are glorified when we show compassion. Help me to never try to absorb glory that belongs to you alone. I pray that you would make me humble and compassionate toward others, and that you would be glorified in my life.

Notes for Resurrection 4: Son of the Widow from Nain

Day 19
[1] R.C. Sproul, https://twitter.com/rcsproul/status/930514265240457218.

Day 20
[2] https://www.google.com/search?q=compassion.
[3] Brown, Driver, and Briggs, *Hebrew Lexicon of the Old Testament*.

Day 21
[4] https://acoustics.org/pressroom/httpdocs/166th/1aAA4_Boren.html.
[5] Ibid.
[6] Scott Duvall. Devotions on the Greek N.T., Page 46.
[7] Ibid, 47.

Day 22
[8] Ryan Gaydos 8/4/21, https://www.foxnews.com/sports/simone-biles-larry-nassar-abuse-tokyo-olympics.
[9] Source: Musixmatch. Songwriter: William J. Gaither. "He Touched Me" lyrics © Hanna Street Music, New Spring Publishing Inc.

.

Resurrection 5

THE DAUGHTER OF JAIRUS

Luke 8:49-56

DAY 25
BELIEVE DURING DESPERATION

And falling at Jesus' feet, he implored him to come to his house (Luke 8:41b).

The Horrible Feeling of Desperation

When I (Daniel) was in the U.S. Army in the 1990s, we were on a deployment rotation to the National Training Center located in Fort Irwin, California. This deployment served as training in the event our unit was deployed to Iraq. During this training event, we would have mock battles using a vast and complex laser-tag-type system. Every vehicle, person, and weapon was equipped with this laser system, including tanks, helicopters, planes, individuals, etc. It was intense.

One evening, we had completed a battle and I had to return to the tactical operations center (TOC) to plan the next one. Due to the intensity and demands of the war-like training, I had not slept in more than 48 hours. So, the driver and gunner of my tank offered to let me sleep while they drove me to the TOC. I eagerly agreed and got some much-needed sleep.

I woke up several hours later and quickly realized we should have already arrived at the TOC. I asked the gunner about the situation, and he sheepishly replied that we were lost. I popped open the hatch to have a look around to see if I could recognize any landmarks. However, the Mojave Desert was blanketed that night by an overcast, starless sky. There was zero illumination. Being in a "combat" situation, we weren't allowed to simply turn on our headlights and drive through the desert. We were lost. I knew I was in trouble. I felt that desperation kick in.

The Soberness of Desperation

When we become desperate, an interesting phenomenon can take place. Certain principles or views can be set aside in that desperate moment. We learn in the book of Luke that Jairus was the "ruler of the synagogue." He was a man of dignity, respect, and position.

We don't know much about Jairus prior to this moment. Being Jewish, he certainly would have engaged in conversations about Jesus and whether or not he could be the Messiah. Of course, the vast majority of the Jewish establishment had already decided that Jesus could not be the Messiah. On one extreme, Jairus could have believed Jesus to be the Messiah but was under a great deal of political pressure because of this view. On the other extreme, he could have been one of the more hostile persons who cried out against Jesus being the Messiah.

Regardless of where Jairus fell on the Jewish spectrum, in this moment he set all of that aside. In his desperation, his politics became secondary. In this moment, his reputation became secondary. He was desperate for his little girl to live. And, based on what he had heard, there was some hope if he could get to Jesus.

The Action of Humble Desperation
His moment comes as Jesus arrives in town. Luke records that they were all waiting for him. Jairus rushes forward and plunges to the ground at Jesus' feet in a humble, desperate attempt to implore Jesus for his aid. What a moment. The most influential man in this town falls at the feet of Jesus in front of everyone. If there had been any question about what Jairus believed and hoped about Jesus, this act answered that question. If some families were curious as to where their synagogue leader stood on the Jesus debate, there was now no question. In Jairus' desperate act, he not only demonstrated to Jesus his faith and hope in him, he also led a town to do the same.

Questions for Day 25
1. When was there a time you came to Jesus in desperation, and he answered?
2. How did Jesus respond?
3. To whom have you told that story? To whom could you tell it?

Prayer for Day 25
Lord Jesus, in my desperate moments, fill me with a faith and confidence in you. Help me not to lose hope but to cling to the hope I have in you. Give me opportunity to tell others the stories of how you have been faithful in my desperate moments.

DAY 26
BELIEVE BECAUSE OF EVIDENCE

She came up behind him and touched the fringe of his garment, and immediately her discharge of blood ceased (Luke 8:44).

An Interesting Interlude
After Luke tells us of Jairus making his way through the crowd and throwing himself down at Jesus' feet to beg him to come and heal his daughter, Luke moves to the encounter with a lady with a bleeding problem. Luke inserts this encounter between when Jesus met Jairus and when Jesus arrived at the house of Jairus. This is not a coincidence. Luke – and the Holy Spirit, who is inspiring Luke – includes this insertion on purpose. And Jesus orchestrates this interlude as well. Not only do we see this struggling lady healed, this happens in the view of Jairus, whose desperation is about to hit an even more intense level when he hears that his daughter has died. He will need this evidence to bolster his faith.

At the End of Her Means
For 12 years, this woman has had this bleeding issue. Not only did this serve as a significant health problem, but her bleeding also created numerous other problems for her – the worst of which was that she was perpetually "unclean" and, therefore, was not allowed in the temple area (Leviticus 15:25). She could not participate at the temple in the feasts and festivals. She could not participate in the sacrifices. No doubt, this resulted in her feeling disconnected not only from her people but from God.

Luke tells us that though this poor woman "had spent all her living on physicians, she could not be healed by anyone." She had spent all her money searching for a remedy. She had gone to all the best doctors and tried all the medicines, herbs, and oils. Nothing helped. She was literally at the end of her means. She had no recourse left. No options remained available, that is, until Jesus came to town.

A Power Transfer
In her own desperation, this lady sought to simply touch the edge of Jesus' robe. However, her desperation was also coupled with faith. The last book in the Old Testament – Malachi – contains a prophecy that says, "But for you who fear my name, the sun of righteousness shall rise with healing in its wings" (Malachi 4:2). The word for "wings" in the Hebrew is the same word used in Numbers 15:38 referring to "tassels." As a result, an expectation grew among the Jewish people that when

Messiah came, just the touch of his tassels would bring healing.[1] So, this lady's desperation and faith resulted in her reaching forward to grab the tassels or fringe of Jesus' robe. When she did, she was healed. Jesus recognizes his power leaving him and going to this lady.

Perhaps you're not so different from this desperate woman who lunged for Jesus. Linda was like this woman. She and her husband desired to have children; however, after 19 years, they had no success. They had tried everything the medical world had to offer. One day at church, she and her husband "lunged" for Jesus. They had no other hope. There were no other options. So, they trusted the whole matter to Christ. Within months, she was pregnant and gave birth to a healthy, brilliant boy. This brilliant boy now has provided Linda and her husband with grandchildren and much happiness. How? Because they lunged out of desperation and faith.

Do you have any desperation? Do you need to lunge for Jesus? Let the story of this woman with a bleeding issue be an encouragement to you. She certainly was an encouragement to Jairus. As he observed Jesus heal this woman, can you imagine how much his faith soared as he hoped for his daughter to be healed as well? He, too, was lunging.

Questions for Day 26
1. In what ways do you need to lunge for Jesus?
2. Through what event did God work powerfully in someone's life and specifically encourage you and build your faith?
3. What is one of your stories where God worked in your life in such a way that it would serve as an encouragement and inspiration to someone else?

Prayer for Day 26
Lord, I am desperate for you. Give me the faith and the realization and the urgency to lunge for you. Work in my life in a way that demonstrates to everyone who knows me that the Lord is working in my life.

DAY 27
BELIEVE IN THE IMPOSSIBLE

While he was still speaking, someone from the ruler's house came and said, "Your daughter is dead; do not trouble the Teacher any more" (Luke 8:49).

The End of a Dream?

Have you ever experienced that moment when you realized one of your dreams just wasn't going to happen? I (Daniel) grew up in Nashville and spent some time there doing ministry as well. During the 1990s, hundreds of people would move to Nashville each week trying to make it in the music industry. Musicians seemed to be a dime a dozen. I met numerous men and women who had come to Nashville to be successes as songwriters, singers, and musicians. Needless to say, there are many unfulfilled dreams in Nashville.

Can you imagine the thoughts and emotions of Jairus when he heard those seemingly hope-ending, dream-shattering words, "Your daughter is dead"? Maybe you can identify. Things seemed to be looking up for Jairus and his daughter as Jesus was heading to his house. Maybe there's been a situation for you where things seemed to be looking better, and then the world came tumbling down. The hope ended. The dream seemed shattered.

God Over the Impossible

Throughout biblical history, God has revealed time and time again that he is all-powerful even over the impossible. He caused Abraham and Sarah to have a child, Isaac, despite their extreme age and the fact that they were biologically past child-bearing ability. God parted the Red Sea so nearly two million Hebrews led by Moses could walk across dry ground and escape the Egyptian army. As we've already seen, God supernaturally fed the widow at Zarephath, her son, and Elijah for weeks from one jar of oil and flour. Jesus was raised from the dead into his glorified body. God does the impossible.

Jairus was doubtless completely deflated. His hopes that Jesus would heal his daughter had vanished. Luke records, however, "But Jesus on hearing this answered him, 'Do not fear; only believe, and she will be well' " (Luke 8:50). For a few brief seconds, Jairus' hope had been destroyed. Yet in those few words from Jesus, "she will be well," his hope's fire was rekindled.

Luke does not give us the thoughts of Jairus in these moments. We don't know if Jairus' faith soared when Jesus said these words or if skepticism filled his mind. Most likely, he had heard about what Jesus had done in Nain at the funeral in Luke 7. So, most likely, his faith began to soar in an instant. What a difference the word from the Lord can make! His is the word of hope and promise.

Power to Promise

When Jesus assured Jairus and the other listeners that this girl would be made well, he was not simply proclaiming empty words. The reason hope soared and the promise was believed was because Jesus had demonstrated he had the power to make those promises into reality. Have you ever unintentionally lied? Have you promised your child you'd be at his ballgame only to get called into a mandatory meeting at work that prevented you from fulfilling your promise? What happened? You did not have the power to guarantee your promise. God is all-powerful. This is why God never lies.

In fact, Hebrews 6:18 says, "it is impossible for God to lie." God cannot lie because he is never powerless to fulfill his promises.

If you're facing some impossible situations right now, what promises from God's word apply to you in this situation? He is God over the impossible! He will never lie. He is faithful, and your faith is believing in his promises and his power to keep those promises.

Questions for Day 27

1. What impossible things, other than those listed earlier, does Scripture say God has done?
2. How would you have responded to Jesus' statement, "she will be well"?
3. Have you seen God do the impossible in your life? How?

Prayer for Day 27

Lord God, I believe you are all-powerful. Forgive me for the times I have doubts or am skeptical about your ability. Lord, show me the promises in your word that I am to hold on to. Thank you for the hope that I always have in you. Lord, build that hope as you build my faith.

DAY 28
BELIEVE IN THE FACE OF THE SCORN

And all were weeping and mourning for her, but he said, "Do not weep, for she is not dead but sleeping." And they laughed at him, knowing that she was dead (Luke 8:52-53).

A Ludicrous Rejection

Have you ever heard of Clifton "Pop" Herring? Most people probably haven't heard of him. After all, he was simply a basketball coach at Laney High School in Wilmington, North Carolina. In the sports world, those that do recognize his name know him as the coach who cut Michael Jordan — the player held by most to be the greatest of all time. Truth be told, Pop invested a great deal in Jordan and only cut him from varsity to junior varsity to give him much more playing time to hone his skills and incredible talent. However, most who know his name equate him with the guy who rejected the best.

I'm sure if we could go back and talk to some of these bystanders just moments after they laughed at Jesus, they would certainly realize how ludicrous their response was. No one wants to be the person known for rejecting the greatest of all time.

Faith Despite Others' Rejection

Jesus remained unwavering in his pursuit to heal this girl. What is more, Jairus makes no attempt to stop Jesus — even after his friends, family, and loved ones are laughing at the ridiculous notion that this girl is merely sleeping. He continued to cling to the words that Jesus had said, "Do not fear; only believe, and she will be well" (Luke 8:50b). There will be circumstances when you find yourself in the minority of those who trust Jesus. In fact, there may be times when you're the only one who trusts in Jesus. How do you navigate those situations? Perhaps you are out with your friends from work, and they are beginning to engage in practices that go against what the Bible teaches. What do you do? You do the same thing Jairus did. You cling to the words of Jesus.

When my (Daniel's) dad was a young teenager, he had just trusted in Jesus. He came from a very poor family — and a really rough family. His extended family was involved in quite a few illegal activities such as bootlegging and running distilleries; he grew up in the Smoky Mountains. The name Carr had quite a few negative associations in the community.

My dad trusted in Christ because of the ministry of a little church in the area called Bethel Baptist Church. No doubt, when my dad trusted in Christ and began to attend services at Bethel, many would have raised an eyebrow at "that Carr kid" being there. However, instead of judging my dad based on his family, they embraced him, loved him, and provided for him. The Lord used this little congregation to love my dad into the kingdom of God.

Bethel Baptist Church knew what Jairus knew: in spite of tough circumstances, you can never go wrong trusting in Jesus. His word is always true, and he can genuinely change anyone – a dead girl into a living girl *and* a young hillbilly from a rough family into a fully devoted follower of Jesus.

So, what do you do when you find yourself in the midst of those who don't believe, and who even ridicule Jesus? You cling to Jesus' words. You listen to the greatest of all time.

Questions for Day 28
1. When was a time you felt like you were the only one in a group that trusted in Jesus? How did you handle it?
2. How can you become equipped to cling to Jesus and his word even when tough circumstances come?
3. Do you know someone currently facing tough circumstances whom you could encourage?

Prayer for Day 28
Lord, thank you that I can always trust you. You will always keep your word. I can always cling to you, even in the midst of terrible situations. Lord, strengthen me to pursue your word and to be equipped to stand strong in the faith – all for your glory!

DAY 29
BELIEVE IN THE AUTHORITY OF JESUS

But taking her by the hand he called, saying, "Child, arise" (Luke 8:54).

The Right to Direct or Decide

Dictionary.com defines "authority" as "the right to control, command, or determine."[2] When I (Daniel) was in the U.S. Army, our battalion was supposed to be getting a new commander. Our former commander was being transferred to a new assignment. One day as I was walking into the battalion headquarters, I noticed a gentleman in civilian clothes coming into the office. As I entered behind him, he was barking orders to one of the enlisted office clerks. I, being an officer, sought to protect this young clerk and intervened. I asked him, "May I help you, sir?" He could tell by my tone I didn't appreciate him coming in and barking orders to our soldiers. He rather sternly informed me that he was the incoming battalion commander (a lieutenant colonel, which is a rather high-ranking field-grade officer). I quickly changed my entire posture and tone, "Yessir, how may I help?"

Jesus' Authority

In almost any other moment like the one with the daughter of Jairus, had anyone said, "Child, arise," there would have been stiff opposition, ridicule, and perhaps even physical violence. However, that is not the case since this is Jesus. If you or I were to attempt calling forth the deceased, we would fail miserably – not because of our lack of care or concern but because of our lack of authority. God – and God alone – has the right and position to command life and death. Jesus, as God in the flesh, has full authority over the life of Jairus' daughter. Just as the new battalion commander had the right to issue orders and for those orders to be obeyed, so Jesus also has the right to issue commands to his creation with the expectation of obedience.

You and I fall under the authority of Jesus. Whether we believe in him or not – whether we worship him or not – we are under his authority. Jesus says in Matthew 28:18, "All authority in heaven and on earth has been given to me." Jesus has the right and the position to command us in our lives. He has the right and the position to expect obedience. Yet, amazingly, when we disobey him, we are not zapped off this planet. We are not immediately killed or hauled off to an eternal prison (which would be just). Why not?

Jesus' Mercy

The reason you and I are still alive and living without being incarcerated by Jesus is because of his mercy and grace – all driven by his love. Mercy is when God does NOT give us what we deserve. We deserve punishment for our disobedience and neglecting his authority. Yet, when Jesus went to the cross, he took our place. He received the just punishment our disobedience deserves. In this way, he is merciful. He, then, also gives us grace. Grace is when God gives us what we DON'T deserve. So, Jesus, who has all authority, grants us both mercy and grace. How should we respond? We should love him back. And how do we show him we love him? Jesus tells us, "If you love me, you will keep my commandments" (John 14:15). We show him our love for him by obeying him. How are you doing at obeying him?

Questions for Day 29

1. Have you ever struggled submitting to someone who had authority over you?
2. Who is someone who had authority over you whom you deeply admired and respected?
3. What was a time when you obeyed Jesus? How did you feel about your obedience?
4. What is Jesus commanding in your life that you are struggling to obey? Why are you struggling?
5. How does understanding that he has the right to command your life and expect obedience change your willingness to obey?

Prayer for Day 29

Lord Jesus, I acknowledge your authority as Lord and King. Forgive me for the many times I have disobeyed you and not honored you and your authority. Please grant me an obedient spirit to you. Help me show you that I love you by my obedience.

DAY 30

And her spirit returned, and she got up at once (Luke 8:55a).

Sheer Power

In my (Daniel) senior year of high school, my football team was playing in Tennessee's state playoffs. This accomplishment was a major milestone because we were the first team from my school to ever go to the playoffs. However, our accomplishment would be short-lived.

We were playing Dickson County High School. They had a running back named Ricky Vaughn, who was being courted by numerous Division I schools. On the opening kickoff, Vaughn received the ball and ran up the middle. In one epic moment, he found himself head-to-head with our best linebacker and defensive player. As I watched from the sideline (I was the quarterback, so I didn't play on the kickoff team), the play seemed to happen in slow motion. As Vaughn and our linebacker ran straight for each another, we all clenched our fists to await this epic moment of two champions facing off. Like two bulls charging, the two athletes sprinted toward each other. As they collided with the crash of their helmets, we helplessly held our breath and unclenched our hands. Vaughn ran right over our linebacker. In fact, I'm not sure he even broke stride. His sheer power was no match for our linebacker (who went on to play in college). On the field that day, Vaughn was the man among boys. We were no match for his power as they annihilated us, 44-6.

As Jesus commanded, "Child, arise!" (Luke 8:54b), death was no match for the sheer power of God in the flesh. He who had spoken the universe into existence now with the same voice called that little girl back to life. Whatever disease had taken hold of her, whatever condition had befallen her, completely crumbled at the power of the Lord's command. Jesus did not require rehearsal or practice. He is the embodiment of the power of the universe.

Total Power

This little girl got up at once. Jesus did not require time to build up his power. He did not have to try to say the exact right words or conduct the right motions. There was no delay. He commanded, and life returned at once. Embracing the reality of the power of Jesus in our faith is absolutely life changing. When Jesus saves us through faith, he has the power to completely save us for all of eternity. Neither our death, our sickness, our sinfulness, our addictions, or our failures are any match for his power. They all crumble under the matchless power of Jesus. The one who called forth the stars into existence is now your Shepherd. He watches over you. He guides you. He protects you. Yet in all his power and might, he loves you. Just as Jesus was moved with compassion for Jairus' daughter, he is moved with compassion for you and your struggles. Take them to Jesus. Paul reminds us in Ephesians 3:20, "Now to [God] who is able to do far more abundantly than all that we ask or think, according to the power at work within us, to him be glory." He is able to protect, to save, and to provide. Trust him.

Questions for Day 30
1. How have you seen God's power at work in your life? In the life of a loved one?
2. How do you need God's power in your life today?
3. What might be keeping you from trusting in God's power in your life?

Prayer for Day 30
Lord, I am amazed at your power and might. I am even more in awe of how much you love me. Increase my faith in you. I give my struggles to you. Although they might be bigger than me, I believe they are no match for you.

Notes for Resurrection 5: The Daughter of Jairus

Day 26
[1] Endofthematter.com/2015/10/why-is-there-healing-in-the-hem-of-jesus-garment/ Updated Sep. 12, 2021.

Day 29
[2] "Authority", www.dictionary.com/browse/authority.

Resurrection 6

LAZARUS

John 11:1-44

DAY 31
ALREADY, BUT NOT YET: INDIFFERENCE OR LOVE?

Now a certain man was ill, Lazarus of Bethany, the village of Mary and her sister Martha (John 11:1).

Indifference Or Love?
It was a terrifying phone call. I (Martin) still remember the details of where I was when I received it. I was working in my barn on our little farm in West Plains, Missouri. My mom called my cell phone and told me that my stepdad had been in an accident. He was blinded by the sun as he rounded a corner on his motorcycle, and he veered from the road and crashed. My mother wasn't sure how bad it was going to be. All she knew was that they loaded him into an ambulance and he was on his way to the hospital. My heart sank. I just knew it was going to be bad. I'm usually the optimist in the room, but this didn't sound good at all. After finding this out, I simply went back to what I was doing in the barn and waited for my wife to yell down to the barn that supper was ready. When I mentioned it to her at the dinner table, we said a quick prayer for him and then began eating. It was a great spaghetti dinner!

Does something seem wrong with the end of the story that I just told you? What's missing? Maybe the same thing that seems to be missing in our story in John 11. The first verse begins by stating that Lazarus, the brother of Mary and Martha, was sick. We aren't sure how sick he is, but we get the idea that it is a pretty big deal. Mary and Martha send word to Jesus by a messenger: "Lord, he whom you love is ill." When Mary and Martha sent this message to Jesus, I'm guessing that they didn't expect what seemed like indifference from Jesus. After all, Jesus "loved" Lazarus. However, instead of rushing off to see his friend and help him, the Bible tells us that Jesus "stayed two days longer in the place where he was." You may be thinking, "With friends like this, who needs enemies?" Somehow, Jesus isn't troubled by his friend's severe illness.

Thankfully
I wasn't totally truthful with you earlier. After hearing that my stepdad had been in a wreck, I quickly jumped in my truck and drove north to see him in the hospital in Farmington, Missouri. I was nervous and praying the entire way to the hospital for God to preserve my stepdad's life. Thankfully – although there were several broken ribs, a punctured lung, and some other minor injuries – God preserved his life. Now, several years later, we are still enjoying his company.

Jesus is God incarnate. His ways are higher than ours. His knowledge is infinite. The fact that he doesn't react the way we would in each situation doesn't mean that he is not in control or does not have a plan. In fact, his plan is always the best plan, whether we want to admit it or not. His time frame of working is also always infinitely perfect. Even though Mary, Martha, and maybe even the disciples of Jesus are going to seem baffled by what seemed to be indifference, Jesus showed himself once again to be the author and sustainer of life.

Jesus Isn't Indifferent

Jesus was taking his time 15-20 miles away from where Lazarus was, because God had a big plan up his sleeve. When the envoy from Mary and Martha tells Jesus that Lazarus is sick, he says, "This illness does not lead to death. It is for the glory of God, so that the Son of God may be glorified through it." Just a few verses later, we see that Lazarus dies. Was Jesus a false prophet, or was Jesus getting ready to do something incredible that would ring down through the corridors of time as one of his greatest miracles? Would an act of grace, power, and mercy validate the ministry of Jesus, or would he be found to be wrong about his friend Lazarus? Often, we go through difficult things in life and wonder why God isn't answering our prayers the way we think he should. The important thing to remember is that he has a plan, and that even though he may seem indifferent, he isn't. He is at work. God is in the same place that he was when his Son was pouring out his life for us on the cross. He is on his throne and working for our good. Indifference and love don't go together. In whatever difficulty you are experiencing, remember Jesus' words, "This illness does not lead to death. It is for the glory of God, so that the Son of God may be glorified through it." He has a plan.

Questions for Day 31

1. How is this story a good example of realizing that God is not indifferent to our pain and suffering?
2. Have you ever felt like God moved slower in answering your prayers than you wished? If so, what were those prayers? What did Mary and Martha think of Jesus moving so slowly?
3. When the news came to Jesus that Lazarus was ill, what did Mary and Martha expect Jesus to do? What did he do instead?
4. Is there pain in your life right now to which it seems God is indifferent? How can this story be a reminder for you today of God's glory?

Prayer for Day 31

Father, help me to be satisfied with your answers to my requests through prayer. Help me to trust that you always have the best in store for me, even if I don't understand it. I pray today that the Son of God would be glorified through my life no matter what path you have for me.

DAY 32
ALREADY, BUT NOT YET: OUR WEAKNESS, GOD'S GLORY

"Our friend Lazarus has fallen asleep, but I go to awaken him." The disciples said to him, "Lord, if he has fallen asleep, he will recover." Now Jesus had spoken of his death, but they thought that he meant taking rest in sleep. Then Jesus told them plainly, "Lazarus has died" (John 11:11b-14).

Good from Tragedy?
It was a tragic day. In 1967, at the tender age of 17, young Joni Eareckson was paralyzed during a diving accident.[1] Joni was a very active person, and this accident was devastating to her and her entire family. No longer could she move about as an average teenager. Even the simplest of tasks became completely impossible for Joni, who was paralyzed from the neck down. How could anything good possibly come about in Joni's life after this terrible accident? After this life-changing event, Joni suffered from depression and questioned the goodness of God. It appeared that this promising young life wouldn't amount to much of anything.

Mary and Martha loved their brother Lazarus deeply. It is easy to see this love come through the pages of Scripture as we read John 11.

After sending messengers to summon Jesus to come heal Lazarus, both Mary and Martha must have breathed a sigh of relief, knowing that Jesus would quickly come to Bethany to heal their brother. In fact, John 11:5 tells us, "Now Jesus loved Martha and her sister and Lazarus." Jesus' next actions would seem like a no-brainer. However, he does the opposite of what we might think. Rather than quickly go to Bethany or send word that Lazarus would be healed, he stays put with his disciples and seemingly ignores the situation. Jesus allows something very bad to happen (the death of Lazarus) without any intervention at all.

Our Walk with God
Many times, during seasons of difficulty, our prayers appear to go unanswered. Rather than hearing from the Lord during these seasons, it seems as though our prayers are met with a door slam followed by the sound of a locked bolt falling into place. What do we do during these seasons? Do we give up and believe that God has it in for us? Do we trust that even though we may not understand now, God has a greater plan for the situation? If we believe the Scriptures, then we know that even though our current "already" isn't what it should be, there is a perfect "not yet" waiting for us. Romans 8:28 says, "And we

know that for those who love God all things work together for good, for those who are called according to his purpose." It can be hard to believe. But even though our situations might be filled with pain and difficulty, the God of heaven and earth will make all things new and redeem what has been lost. It is important for us to remember that "God is light, and in him there is no darkness at all" (1 John 1:5). Our situation may be dark, but we serve a God who shines light into the darkness.

Beauty for Ashes

Nine years after Joni's ordeal, she released a book. The autobiography *Joni* became a number one bestseller, eventually translated into more than 38 languages with more than 5 million copies in print.[2] Instead of becoming angry at God, Joni turned to him in great faith, and God has used her to reach millions with the gospel. Today, Joni is 72 years old and continues to minister and bring the hope of the gospel all over the world. Joni has an international ministry that has allowed her to share her story and God's goodness on the same platforms as people like Billy Graham. She has written more than 50 books and encouraged millions to trust Jesus as their Lord.

Even though her tragedy would seem to put a unique end to her service for God, it only heightened her ability to reach the world for Jesus. If God is already using Joni in such a unique way, think about the "not yet" that God will use her for in heaven. In 1996, Crystal Lewis wrote a song, "Beauty for Ashes," with the chorus line,

> *He gives beauty for ashes*
> *strength for fear,*
> *gladness for mourning*
> *peace for despair.*

Mary, Martha, the disciples of Jesus, and the entire town of Bethany are about to receive peace for despair from the only one who can give it: Jesus, the Messiah. Because of his mighty power, the small town of Bethany will be famous until his return.

Questions for Day 32

1. What happened to Joni as a teenager that dramatically changed her life?
2. Instead of giving up, what did Joni do with her life?
3. Do you think that Joni's reach with the gospel would have been the same if her accident hadn't happened?
4. When tragedy has caused you to experience difficult seasons in your faith, have you drifted further from God or grown closer to him? Where are you now with that past situation?
5. Do you believe that God can bring beauty from ashes? Have you ever seen him do so?

Prayer for Day 32

Thank you, Lord, for people like Joni who never give up trusting in you. I pray that no matter what difficulties await me in the future, you would give me the grace to trust and grow as Joni did. I thank you, Lord, that you can bring beauty from ashes.

DAY 33

ALREADY, BUT NOT YET: "FOR YOUR SAKE"

The disciples said to him, "Lord, if he has fallen asleep, he will recover." Now Jesus had spoken of his death, but they thought that he meant taking rest in sleep. Then Jesus told them plainly, "Lazarus has died, and for your sake I am glad that I was not there, so that you may believe. But let us go to him" (John 11:12-15).

Have You Ever Noticed?

Have you ever noticed in the New Testament the disciples are sometimes confused by what Jesus says? At times it even seems as though Jesus is toying with them. He speaks in parables that they don't understand and many times says things that, quite frankly, don't make any sense to them until later. Following are a few such passages from Mark's Gospel, for instance: Mark 4:40; 6:51-52; 8:4, 14-21; 8:33; 9:2-10; 14:68-72. Jesus begins to do the same thing here in John 11. He speaks of Lazarus as having "fallen asleep." The disciples respond to Jesus without a care in the world, claiming that if Lazarus is merely asleep, then he will recover! Jesus finally tells the disciples plainly, "Lazarus has died." Jesus makes it crystal clear that Lazarus is a corpse.

Meanwhile, in Bethany

After Lazarus' death, there would have been great mourning in the community. The body, according to Jewish tradition (Mishnah Sanhedrin 6:6), must be buried the day that death occurs.[3] While the entire town would have been in mourning, there was work to be done. Lazarus' body had to be washed with perfumes and ointments. His body was wrapped tightly and bound with strips of cloth.[4] We know this tradition was followed closely because John says that Lazarus' hands, feet, and face were all wrapped with strips of cloth. After one year of being in this state, Lazarus' body would have been taken out of the burial cloths, and his bones would have been put inside an ossuary. For Mary, Martha, and the town of Bethany, Lazarus' story was ending in the most disappointing of ways. It was ending with Jesus, seemingly distracted, just a day's journey away. Not only this, but the sisters would not get to see Jesus until the fourth day after Lazarus had been dead. They must have felt both hurt and confused.

"For Your Sake I Am Glad"

As Jesus reveals to his disciples that Lazarus is truly dead, he tells them that he is glad and says it happened "so that you may believe." Instead of being afraid of what they would find when they went to Bethany – Lazarus dead and an entire town grieving – Jesus says clearly, "Lazarus has died, and for your sake I am glad that I was not there, so that you may believe. But let us go to him." It seems obvious that Jesus has a surprise up his sleeve for everyone involved in this tragedy. Jesus isn't concentrating on the "already" (Lazarus being dead) but instead has his eyes fixed on the "not yet" (a coming miracle).

As Jesus comes to Bethany, he witnesses the deep grief over the tragedy of Lazarus. "Bethany was near Jerusalem, about two miles off, and many of the Jews had come to Martha and Mary to console them concerning their brother. So when Martha heard that Jesus was coming, she went and met him, but Mary remained seated in the house." Probably both grief and maybe a little resentment kept Mary seated inside the house as Jesus came into town.

"So That You May Believe"
Jesus didn't answer the call right away when he heard about Lazarus. He purposefully delayed and allowed his friend to die, so a greater cause could be fulfilled. As we saw yesterday in the reading about Joni, we see again that the master plan of God will always work toward our good, even when we can't see it. The death of Lazarus is going to bring about the faith of many. Jesus tells his disciples that the purpose of the Lazarus situation is "so that you may believe." This Lazarus event is just two weeks or so before Jesus is killed on the cross. Before that cataclysmic event, the disciples are going to need to see a miracle.

Questions for Day 33
1. What is different about an ancient Jewish burial from American custom?
2. What happens to the bones of the Hebrew deceased one year after burial?
3. If you were a disciple of Jesus, do you think you would have been confused by him saying, "Lazarus is dead, and for your sake I am glad I wasn't there"? Does that seem cold?
4. When difficulty comes, do you think of stories like this to remind you of God's larger purpose that might not be evident during the difficulty?
5. When Jesus arrived, do you believe that Mary stayed seated over grief, or do you think she was a little upset with Jesus for not coming sooner? (Obviously we can't know for sure, but what do you think?)

Prayer for Day 33
Father, help me to know that during difficult situations you show up right on time. You have a plan, and it's always good. Help me to trust you more and to recognize that during hard times, you are still on your throne working all things out according to the purpose of your will.

DAY 34

ALREADY, BUT NOT YET: THE FINAL ENEMY TO BE DEFEATED

Now when Jesus came, he found that Lazarus had already been in the tomb four days (John 11:17).

Death?

Death is terrible, isn't it? It is also certain. Every person on the planet today will at some point in their future face physical death unless Jesus comes back first. The Bible tells us that the "wages of sin is death." We have all earned it by being born in sin (Romans 5:12). The Bible also says that "the last enemy to be destroyed is death." I think it is the finality of death that hurts so bad. When someone dies, that's it. There are no more apologies that you can make. There is no way to take back any hurtful words. There is no more "I love you." It's simply over. Communication with that person is gone, never to be regained again in this life.

But What Exactly Is Death?

While even medical scholars disagree on what exactly constitutes death, it seems as though there is general agreement that "clinical death is the medical term for cessation of blood circulation and breathing, the two necessary criteria to sustain human and many other organisms' lives. It occurs when the heart stops beating in regular rhythm, a condition called cardiac arrest."[5] We all know death when we see it, don't we? After death, a condition referred to as rigor mortis affects the body. This condition makes the body stiff and stuck in position. Lazarus experienced all these conditions. His heart stopped. His brain function ceased. His body was locked in rigor mortis. He was prepped and wrapped for burial before the day was out, and he was placed behind a burial stone. The enemy – death – visited Bethany that sad day.

"He Has Been Dead Four Days"

Jesus, just a few miles away, attempts to make it clear that the death of Lazarus has not come as a surprise to him. He even tells the disciples that, for their sake, he is glad that he was not there in Bethany to prevent it. In fact, Jesus doesn't get to Bethany until four days after the death of Lazarus. As Jesus arrives, the grief amongst the people is still very fresh. Martha runs out to greet Jesus.

"Then Jesus, deeply moved again, came to the tomb. It was a cave, and a stone lay against it. Jesus said, 'Take away the stone.' Martha, the sister of the dead man, said to him, 'Lord, by this time there will be an odor, for he has been dead four days'" (John 11:38-39).

Dead bodies are gross, aren't they? That's why we must bury them! While we aren't used to seeing human corpses lie around, we have probably all seen a dead animal on the side of the road. They puff up, become distorted, and begin to rot. This, of course, causes them to put off a horrible odor. Martha might be thinking that Jesus – who has just wept over his friend (11:35) – is distraught and not thinking logically. Maybe he has forgotten that four days after death, the smell will be terrible. Lazarus' body has begun decomposition, and no matter how badly Jesus wants to see his friend, Martha is just sure this is a bad idea.

The Final Enemy WILL Be Destroyed

Now we begin to see why it has taken Jesus quite a bit of time to land in Bethany. After four days, there is no doubt that Lazarus is dead. There can be no questions left in the minds of those present before Jesus does what he has in his mind to do.

While death seems so final, we are reminded in 1 Corinthians 15:26, "The last enemy to be destroyed is death." How can this ancient foe of humanity (and the whole world) be defeated by God in the last times? How can we be assured of such things? Words aren't enough, are they? Sometimes we need to see the proof of Jesus' words. Of course, Jesus never disappoints.

Questions for Day 34

1. Why does death seem so final?
2. When you think of death, how have you typically defined it? Brain function has ceased? Heart stops beating? Both?
3. What would have happened to Lazarus' body after being in the tomb four days? What does Martha warn Jesus about?
4. What does the Bible say about death being the final enemy?
5. What does the Bible say we have earned for our sin? The wages of sin is _____. Is that the end of the story?

Prayer for Day 34

Father, I thank you that the final enemy, death, will be destroyed. I thank you for the love of Jesus toward his friend Lazarus and that through the gospel, I am no longer an enemy of God but a friend. Thank you, Father, that Jesus never disappoints!

DAY 35
ALREADY, BUT NOT YET: DOWN PAYMENT

Jesus said to her, "Your brother will rise again." Martha said to him, "I know that he will rise again in the resurrection on the last day." Jesus said to her, "I am the resurrection and the life. Whoever believes in me, though he die, yet shall he live, and everyone who lives and believes in me shall never die. Do you believe this?" She said to him, "Yes, Lord; I believe that you are the Christ, the Son of God, who is coming into the world" (John 11:23-27).

Just a Little Taste
When I (Martin) was a kid growing up, I had a definite sweet tooth. I remember that my mom didn't want any of us eating sweets before supper. However, there was a small part of her that wasn't quite so militant. Even though the brownies – or whatever she made as a sweet treat – were to remain untouched until after the meal, my sister or I would often get to clean the bowl that had the remaining batter in it before dinner began. This little foretaste of what was coming later would get us excited enough to eat our greens so we could bite into that delicious, delectable brownie after supper. This pre-dessert treat was like a small down payment that left us in anticipation of what was coming after supper.

Life in Christ and the Down Payment
When I became a Christian, I didn't become perfect. If you know me, you know that's true. But you didn't become perfect either. The moment we became believers in the gospel, we received the foreign righteousness of Jesus on our lives. We didn't become righteous, but instead, when we believed the gospel, the righteousness of Christ was credited to our account. But our lives began to change as well. While perfection will never be grasped by you or me on this side of heaven, we did receive the gift of the Holy Spirit and began the process of sanctification. Sanctification is God making sinners holy in heart and conduct. Our change is proof that God has done something radical in our lives. Even though we aren't perfect, the change that the Spirit brings in our lives is a sweet taste for us of what total and complete fellowship will be one day in heaven with Jesus. Paul says in Ephesians 1:14, "The Holy Spirit is the down payment on our inheritance, which is applied toward our redemption as God's own people, resulting in the honor of God's glory." If you have not tasted that liberating freedom that comes through believing the gospel and being filled with God's Spirit, you can do that today by fully turning in faith to Jesus.

Martha Knows Jesus' Theology

Martha doesn't know that the entire town of Bethany is going to experience a down payment of God's promises that will be fulfilled on the last day. Jesus has already taught his disciples that there will be a future resurrection as a part of the last day. In fact, just a few chapters earlier in John 6, Jesus said to those to whom he was preaching, "For I have come down from heaven, not to do my own will but the will of him who sent me. And this is the will of him who sent me, that I should lose nothing of all that he has given me, but raise it up on the last day. For this is the will of my Father, that everyone who looks on the Son and believes in him should have eternal life, and I will raise him up on the last day."

Then "Jesus said to her, 'Your brother will rise again.' " Martha thinks that Jesus is referencing the future event at the end of the world and says, "I know that he will rise again in the resurrection on the last day." However, Jesus has a foretaste of the sweetness that the resurrection day will be like in his mind. Jesus is getting ready to show the people of Bethany who really controls life and death. He says to Martha, "I am the resurrection and the life. Whoever believes in me, though he die, yet shall he live, and everyone who lives and believes in me shall never die" (John 11:23-26).

This isn't dessert time (the last day), but this is going to be cleaning the bowl of ingredients before dinner (a foretaste of dessert).

Questions for Day 35

1. Did you have a mixing bowl experience as a kid? How did it make you feel about the final dessert?
2. Who does Ephesians say is the down payment for those who trust in Jesus?
3. How have you seen the Holy Spirit change you after you trusted in Jesus?
4. Think of a time when you felt God's presence through the Holy Spirit and been encouraged. How could that be a taste of what eternity with Jesus will be like?

Prayer for Day 35

Father, I thank you for providing the Holy Spirit as a guide and encouragement. Thank you for giving me a taste of your goodness and helping me look forward to what eternity with you will be like. Help me to recognize and appreciate your presence each day.

DAY 36
ALREADY, BUT NOT YET: CERTAINTY IS COMING

When he had said these things, he cried out with a loud voice, "Lazarus, come out." The man who had died came out, his hands and feet bound with linen strips, and his face wrapped with a cloth. Jesus said to them, "Unbind him, and let him go" (John 11:43-44).

Passion Week

With passion week right around the corner for Jesus, this will be the most incredible miracle to date demonstrating the power of Jesus. If Jewish tradition were being followed in the first six resurrections, every person we've profiled so far would have been buried the same day that they physically died. The stories all seem to indicate this as well. None of the previous stories indicates that any of the resurrections came after the deceased was already laid behind a stone for several days. As I pointed out in the last couple of readings, Lazarus has been dead for four days. This fact is an anomaly in the stories up to this point, and, in my opinion, indicative of the fact that Jesus is saving the best miracle for last in his earthly ministry. Waiting four days ensures that there is no doubt as to the death of Lazarus. He is gone, and there is no turning back time.

"Lazarus, Come Out!"

When Jesus speaks, even the dead listen. Jesus calls to a dead man, and the dead man awakens! Again, this is a preview of the resurrection day that is in the future. This demonstrates that everything that Christ has said will happen in the future is a definite thing. Just as Jesus cried out with a loud voice and his dead friend obeyed, all the saints who are now with Jesus will experience the same thing. Earlier in John 5, Jesus said, "Do not marvel at this, for an hour is coming when all who are in the tombs will hear his voice and come out, those who have done good to the resurrection of life, and those who have done evil to the resurrection of judgment." Martin Luther understood the power of Jesus' voice in calling the dead to life in his great song, "A Mighty Fortress Is Our God." Verse three says,

> The prince of darkness grim,
> we tremble not for him;
> his rage we can endure,
> for lo his doom is sure;
> **one little word** shall fell him.

The power of Jesus' words in the story of Lazarus is just a preview of what will come later. Let's parse this out a little more.

The Resurrection to Come

As great as this story is, Lazarus is going to die again, isn't he? I mean, he isn't around today testifying to Jesus' resurrection power, is he? That is why both Daniel and I refer to these six incredible moments in Scripture as "resuscitations" rather than true resurrections. These six acts are more like down payments that help us to know and believe there is a time in the future when death is completely abolished through an eternal resurrection.

When Martha referred to the resurrection that will happen on the last day, she is referring to a time when death will truly and ultimately be destroyed and banished forever. At that time in the future, each believer will be transformed from death to eternal life in a glorified body (1 Thess. 4; 1 Cor. 15). Paul tells us in 1 Corinthians 15:52 that this will happen "in the twinkling of an eye." He also tells us in Philippians 3 that "our citizenship is in heaven, and from it we await a Savior, the Lord Jesus Christ, who will transform our lowly body to be like his glorious body, by the power that enables him even to subject all things to himself." This is not what Lazarus experienced. If Lazarus had received a resurrected body like Jesus', his physical body would have never died again. However, this temporary resuscitation demonstrates the power of Jesus over both sin and death and testifies to the reality of a future time when restoration will happen in both the spiritual and physical realms. Jesus' resurrection will be the prototype of what we will experience on the last day. His ultimate miracle is raising himself from the dead.

Who Is Going to Raise Jesus from the Dead?

You probably answered this question by saying, "God, of course!" True, but one clear way to see that Jesus is God in human form is to see that Jesus prophesied that he would raise himself from the dead.

The book of Acts tells the history of the early church and how churches were planted as the gospel spread. The main thrust of the teaching of the early church was that God raised Jesus. In Acts 2:32, Peter says, "This Jesus God raised up again, to which we are all witnesses…" While preaching to a man named Cornelius, Peter says in Acts 10:40, "God raised him up on the third day and granted that he become visible…" And in Acts 17:30-31, the apostle Paul says, "God is now declaring to men that all people everywhere should repent, because he has fixed a day in which he will judge the world in righteousness through a man whom he has appointed, having furnished proof to all men by raising him from the dead." These passages make it clear that the teaching of the early church was that God alone is the one who raised Jesus.

Yet Jesus predicts raising himself from the dead in John's Gospel. "Jesus answered them, 'Destroy this temple, and in three days I will raise it up.' The Jews then said, 'It took forty-six years to build this temple, and will you raise it up in three days?' But he was speaking of the temple of his body" (John 2:19-21).

Prepare yourselves for no mere resuscitation but for the true resurrection from the dead in the person of Jesus. A foretaste of what we will experience in glory!

Questions for Day 36
1. What is the difference between Lazarus' resuscitation and the five previous to him?
2. Why do the authors refer to the six raisings as being resuscitations rather than resurrections?
3. How did Lazarus' resuscitation differ from what will happen on the last day to believers in Jesus?
4. Why would Jesus' resurrected body be referred to as the prototype for us?
5. What does Philippians 3 say will happen to our bodies in the future if we are believers in the gospel?
6. Who raised Jesus from the dead: himself or God? Trick question.

Prayer for Day 36
Lord Jesus, thank you for raising yourself from the dead! We thank you for the story of Lazarus that demonstrates that you can raise a rotting corpse up and give it life! We pray that you would help us be diligent to spread the good news of the gospel to as many as possible, so they can receive new life in you and a resurrection of life as well.

———————————————

Notes for Resurrection 6: Lazarus

Day 32
[1] https://www.joniandfriends.org/about/our-history/.
[2] Ibid.

Day 33
[3] https://www.sefaria.org/Mishnah_Sanhedrin.6.5?lang=bi.
[4] R. McCane Byron. https://www.Bibleodyssey.org/en/people/related-articles/burial-practices-in-first-century-palestine.

Day 34
[5] Rachel Nuwer, *Smart News*, https://www.smithsonianmag.com/smart-news/whats-the-difference-between-clinically-dead-figuratively-dead-and-just-plain-dead-129851139/.

Resurrection 7

JESUS' RESURRECTION

John 20:1-18

DAY 37
VICTORY OVER DESPAIR

Early on the first day of the week, while it was still dark, Mary Magdalene went to the tomb (John 20:1a).

Congratulations. You've made it to this final – and most important – week. This week we will journey through the historical account of the resurrection of Jesus. As both Martin and I (Daniel) have already mentioned, the resurrection of Jesus is really the only true resurrection to date. The other six we've discussed were actually resuscitations where the raised would eventually die again. But not Jesus. He is alive! He arose to life to never die again – ever. So, as you read this week, do so with the utmost of worship, celebration, and rejoicing. We serve the risen, living Christ!

A New Direction Denied
We don't know a great deal of Mary Magdalene prior to meeting Jesus. According to Luke 8, she was from the town of Magdala and Jesus had cured her of seven evil spirits and diseases. Many have speculated that she was a prostitute, identifying her as the sinful woman in Luke 7 who washed Jesus' feet with her tears and hair. However, the Bible gives no reason to make that assumption. In New Testament times, demon possession was an indication of physical and spiritual sickness. Obviously, Mary had been quite ill prior to Jesus healing her.

Mary had left everything to follow Jesus. Luke 8 even reveals that she, along with some other women, supported Jesus financially out of their own means. She was all in. She had met Jesus. He loved her, healed her, and now led her. She followed, believing him to be the Messiah. But things had not progressed as she thought they would. None of the disciples expected their leader, the Messiah and Son of God, would be killed. How had it come to this?

Why had she given up everything and followed him? What would she do now? How do you start over after such a powerful journey that offered so much hope and potential? Her new direction seemed to have come to an end.

Love Continues to Serve
Amazingly, Mary maintained a high degree of love and loyalty to Jesus. On this particular Sunday morning, she is going to participate, along with other women including Jesus' own mother Mary, in the anointing of Jesus' body with spices (Mark 16:1). Even though her hope for

the future had been obliterated, she still loved Jesus and wanted to honor him. She was going to help apply the spices to his corpse. This speaks volumes of Mary's love. Love serves even when circumstances seem bleak. Mary did not allow her despair to turn her inward. That is our natural tendency. When we are sick, suffering, hurting, or when our dreams are shattered, we want to turn inward and bathe in our sorrows. But, following Mary's example, let's not do this. Let's choose to be selfless and serve others even in our own trials and struggles.

Love Lives and Obliterates Despair

As we read in John 20, Mary sees the tomb open and runs to get Peter and John in her panic. As they investigate, Mary stands outside the tomb weeping. She sees two angels and asks them where Jesus' body is. She then sees Jesus but assumes him to be the gardener. Jesus asks her a question, but her despair continues to prevent her from truly seeing, hearing, and understanding this is Jesus. Finally, when Jesus says her name, "Mary," she is launched out of her despair and into the realization of renewed and greater hope.

Isn't it amazing how Mary was so in the depths of despair she either did not recognize the two angels as angels or did not care, and she did not recognize Jesus or his voice. She was blinded by her despair. Yet Jesus in his grace continues to pursue her, even to call her name. In our seasons of despair, never forget that Jesus lives! He loves you. He calls you by name. Don't let your despair drown out what Jesus is doing in your life.

Questions for Day 37

1. Describe a time when you were in such despair that it drowned out the work of the Lord in your life.
2. What can you do today that will help you maintain hope in Christ the next time you are tempted to despair?
3. How can you encourage someone else today to have hope?

Prayer for Day 37

Lord Jesus, thank you that you never leave me and never forsake me. Thank you that you are alive and we have all hope in you. Forgive me of those times I despair and lose my focus on trusting in you. Continue to build my faith and hope and confidence in you.

DAY 38
VICTORY OVER CONFUSION

They have taken the Lord out of the tomb, and we do not know where they have laid him (John 20:2b).

Things Are Not Always as They Seem
The D-Day invasion of Allied troops into Normandy has gone down in history as perhaps the most successful invasion of an occupied territory against great odds of all time. General Dwight D. Eisenhower and his staff of officers from Allied nations excelled in the planning and deliberation that went into this attack. However, this attack almost did not happen. Ike had much resistance, even from Winston Churchill, over aspects of this plan. In fact, their disagreements reached a point where Ike actually communicated with President Roosevelt that he would resign if this matter wasn't resolved. Churchill relented.

General Eisenhower thought things were so bad and hopeless that he almost quit. Obviously, things were not as bad as they seemed. The same was true that Sunday morning when Mary Magdalene first came to the empty tomb. When confronted with the reality that Jesus' body was not in the tomb, she jumped to the conclusion that someone had removed the body without telling the family.

Lack of Understanding, Uncertainty
Dictionary.com defines the word "confusion" as meaning, "lack of understanding; uncertainty." This definition accurately explains Mary's state of mind when she first encountered the empty tomb. She had no category of thought except that someone had removed his body. Her confusion continued as she sees two angels. In spite of these two angels being dressed in white, she remains locked in her confusion. Finally, she sees and hears Jesus but, due to her confusion, mistakes him as the gardener until he calls her name. She greatly lacked understanding.

In 1995 my (Daniel's) grandfather passed away from complications of Alzheimer's disease. Physically, he was a healthy 84-year-old farmer, but his mind had been taken over by this horrific disease. As the disease persisted, his confusion grew more severe and continuous. One day my dad, Gene, went to visit him. They talked for about two hours – laughing, telling stories from the 1930s and 1940s. Then my grandfather looked my dad in the eyes and said, "You know, I sure like talking to you. You should meet my son Gene. You two would get along great." My grandfather had been talking to my dad – his son – for two hours and did not recognize him. He was confused.

Not the God of Confusion
The apostle Paul writes in 1 Corinthians 14:33, "For God is not the God of confusion but of peace." When Jesus calls Mary by her name, she seems to be jolted out of her confusion and into reality. The fog lifted, the skies cleared, and she now had understanding. She now completely understands that Jesus is alive and is standing before her. She responds with, "*Rabboni!*" ("teacher" in Aramaic) and she clings to his feet.

It is amazing and tragic how confused we can become about God and other topics. Our culture is confused when it comes to sex and sexuality. Where there is confusion, that confusion does not come from God. We need the voice of Jesus calling us out by name. We need that moment when the resurrected Jesus calls us out of our confused stupor and jolts us into his reality where we can see him clearly.

Questions for Day 38
1. When was a time you were confused about something and God helped clear it up?
2. What is an issue you see our culture is confused about and how would you answer that confusion biblically?
3. Who do you need to pray for that is in confusion?

Prayer for Day 38
Lord Jesus, thank you that you are not the God of confusion but of peace. I pray that you would continue to grow me in your word so that I can be better protected from confusion. And Lord, wake up our culture to your word and truth. Take away our collective confusion and give us your peace.

DAY 39
VICTORY OVER LOSS

Sir, if you have carried him away, tell me where you have laid him, and I will take him away (John20:15).

The Grief of Loss
I (Daniel) will never forget those long but few hours on March 10, 2021. They had given my dad no hope and had disconnected his ventilator. His oxygen numbers plummeted quickly, but he continued to labor in breathing for a couple of hours while my brother and I stood beside him. My mom was too feeble and weak to be in the hospital room, so she was at home. Even though my brother and I had no doubts of my dad's faith, watching your hero's spirit struggle to leave his body is brutal to witness.

In those moments I felt the sting of death – much like Mary Magdalene felt centuries earlier. She was beside herself with grief as she pleaded for the Lord's body. Where could he be? It was bad enough that she had to watch him die on the cross, but then she even lost his body. She longed to anoint his body with spices and see his hands one last time – those hands that had touched her and healed her of her seven demons. She would see his feet one last time, which had walked beside hers for miles and miles. Perhaps she could see his eyes one last time – those eyes that saw straight through to her soul. She was desperate. She was hurting. She was grieved.

Finality
Death seems so final, so cold. We buried my dad in a traditional casket and cemetery plot. As they closed the casket after the funeral service, I remember thinking, "I won't see him again in this life." As we walked outside and drove the short distance to the cemetery, it was a cold March day. We watched as they lowered his casket into that ground. Then the groundskeepers shoveled the dirt on top of his casket and covered it. It all seemed so final.

The burial of Jesus was most likely not very different. Once that stone was rolled into place and locked, there was a finality to it. They thought they would not see Jesus again. The movement seemed over. Life suddenly seemed to lose its meaning. Finality.

A Prototype

In the moment of Jesus saying, "Mary," that finality disappeared. The moment John and Peter ran into the empty tomb and John then remembered and "believed" (John 20:8). Everything changed in those moments. The finality of death was erased. Despair was replaced with hope. Lost purpose was restored with renewed passion. Mourning turned into dancing. Jesus is alive; he's not gone.

Jesus' resurrection is sometimes referred to as "firstfruits." Paul writes this: "But in fact Christ has been raised from the dead, the firstfruits of those who have fallen asleep" (1 Corinthians 15:20).

This means that just like Jesus was raised from the dead, so will all of us who trust in him. Jesus conquered death once for all – defeating sin and our great enemy, death. Paul says it like this:

"Death is swallowed up in victory. O death, where is your victory? O death, where is your sting? The sting of death is sin, and the power of sin is the law. But thanks be to God, who gives us the victory through our Lord Jesus Christ" (1 Corinthians 15:54b-57).

Because of Jesus, I know my dad is not a loss but just a pause. I know my dad lives. Because Jesus conquered death, all those who have faith in him do as well. Therefore, I look forward to seeing Dad again. Because of Jesus, death is not a finality; it is a graduation to that which is next and, for believers, better. In a moment, my dad trusted in Jesus as Lord and Savior. In a moment, you can, too.

Questions for Day 39

1. How does the reality of the resurrection help you deal with the topic of death?
2. Have you had that life-changing moment when you've decided to follow Jesus?
3. In addition to Jesus, who do you look most forward to being reunited with in glory?

Prayer for Day 39

Lord Jesus, I praise you that because of your resurrection, we have the hope of reunion with you and those we know and love who were your followers as well. Give me hope and victory over the sting of loss. Help me not to live in grief, but in triumph and hope.

DAY 40
VICTORY OVER SIN

Jesus said to her, "Do not cling to me, for I have not yet ascended to the Father" (John 20:17a)

Trapped
When I (Daniel) was a young teenager, I collected baseball cards. I loved them! I would get with my friends and trade them, go to the baseball-card store and barter with the shop owner, and use all my money from mowing yards to buy them. I amassed quite a collection. One day I struck gold. My back-door neighbors had a boy my age named Jack. We were just becoming friends as he was newer to the neighborhood. I was telling him about my baseball-card collection and he said that his older brother had collected for a short period of time and that, although his brother had moved out and was on his own, his old box of cards remained in Jack's house. He asked if I wanted to see them. I responded, "Absolutely!" He brought me the box of cards and offered that I could take them home overnight and look through them. So I did.

As I opened the box and started to go through his cards, I was so excited. These were cards from the 1960s and early 1970s. These were 10+ years older than my cards and more valuable. Players like Mickey Mantle, Willie Mays, and Bob Gibson highlighted the cards in the box. Suddenly, I was overcome with a desire to keep them. I couldn't give these precious cards back. After all, Jack had said he did not really care for the cards. His brother had abandoned them; Jack wouldn't even know. So, I removed them and put those amazing cards into my own boxes. The next day I returned the box to Jack, minus a few cards. But he wouldn't notice, would he? For the next few days, I was nervous he would notice and call me out, so I avoided him. I had become trapped.

Bondage
The fact that Jesus tells Mary he's about to go be with the Father demonstrates that Jesus has indeed conquered sin. Sin is not able to withstand the powerful, pure presence of the Holy God. The reason we are in such bondage is due to sin. Our sin separates us from the benevolent goodness of God. Scripture uses bondage as an image for our sin. Everything, from the Jews being slaves in Egypt to when Babylon destroys Jerusalem and carries the Jews into captivity, serves as a metaphor for the bondage we have in sin. We are helpless against sin. Paul says, "For all have sinned and fall short of the glory of God"

(Romans 3:23). He also says, "And you were dead in the trespasses and sins" (Ephesians 2:1). Dead people are incapable of acting for themselves. Since we were dead in our sins, someone had to act on our behalf. That was Jesus.

It Is Finished

When Jesus was crucified, the Bible records seven different statements he made from the cross. One of those statements was, "It is finished!" After reading this, one easily asks the question, "What is finished?" Jesus had completed the necessary requirement for the atonement of our sin. Because of what Jesus did on the cross, we can now be forgiven. Jesus fulfilled the sacrificial obligation our sins demanded. The apostle Peter says this: "For Christ also suffered once for sins, the righteous for the unrighteous, that he might bring us to God, being put to death in the flesh but made alive in the Spirit" (1 Peter 3:18).

Jesus was victorious over our sin on the cross. As Paul writes: "And you, who were dead in your trespasses and the uncircumcision of your flesh, God made alive together with him, having forgiven us all our trespasses, by canceling the record of debt that stood against us with its legal demands. This he set aside, nailing it to the cross" (Colossians 2:13-14).

Because of Jesus, we now have victory over our sin. The penalty has been paid. God's justice has been satisfied and we can be completely forgiven.

In the days following the stealing of my friend's cards, I was so convicted of my sin – my greed, coveting, stealing, lying, etc. Finally, I just couldn't deal with the heavy conviction from the Holy Spirit any further. I went to Jack's house and knocked on his door. He answered, and I immediately told him I had kept some of his brother's valuable cards for myself and handed him the cards. I was expecting a punch in the face or a harsh scolding from my friend. However, in his graciousness, he said, "You can have them – my gift to you." Jack and I grew to be great friends. Isn't that like Jesus? Our guilt and conviction bring us to confess to Jesus. But, instead of condemning us, he gives us his great gift – forgiveness, reconciliation, and eternal life. He paid for it.

Questions for Day 40

1. Are there sins in your life or from your past you question if God has forgiven?
2. Have you ever asked Jesus to forgive you?
3. If Jesus has conquered our sins, why do you think sometimes we still wrestle with sinful actions, thoughts, and attitudes?

Prayer for Day 40

Lord Jesus, thank you for your forgiveness. Thank you for dying in my place so that I may know you, be saved from the penalty of my sins, and live with you and for you forever!

DAY 41
VICTORY OVER SATAN

He shall bruise your head, and you shall bruise his heel (Genesis 3:15).

War

Poet Eve Merriam once said, "I dream of giving birth to a child who will ask, 'Mother, what was war?'" War has been a reality in God's beautiful creation since the beginning of Satan. Satan introduced Adam and Eve, the first humans, to the concept of rebellion against God. Unfortunately, they bought Satan's lies. When doling out consequences, God prophesied and promised the serpent that the offspring of the woman would ultimately bruise or crush the head of Satan. This prophecy in Genesis 3:15 is known as the first gospel. God promises the day will come when a human will destroy Satan. Jesus' coming, life, death, and resurrection has accomplished Satan's defeat and has set in motion his ultimate destruction.

Battles Continue

Even though Jesus has defeated Satan, the adversary is still around: tempting, deceiving, distorting. This is why so many of the New Testament writers encourage believers to live (walk) in the Spirit. Satan, our flesh, and the world all pull us towards living as though Jesus failed – to live in ways dishonoring to God. But we know Jesus didn't fail – and Satan knows, too. He knows his days are numbered. Jesus is King – not Satan. Jesus is Lord – not Satan. Every day we live to honor Jesus brings glory to Jesus and reminds Satan of his looming destruction. Until that destruction, we face battles every day: decisions, temptations, and relationships that could lead us down a destructive road. This is why Paul teaches us:

"Finally, be strong in the Lord and in the strength of his might. Put on the whole armor of God, that you may be able to stand against the schemes of the devil. For we do not wrestle against flesh and blood, but against the rulers, against the authorities, against the cosmic powers over this present darkness, against the spiritual forces of evil in the heavenly places" (Ephesians 6:10-12).

After the Germans surrendered in World War II, the American soldiers celebrated that the war was over. However, they learned that although the war was over, conflicts and battles remained. The Germans had holdout forces that still led to skirmishes. The German countryside was greatly damaged, and much effort had to go into rebuilding and restoring homes, towns, and businesses. Germany was in political shambles needing a great deal of help to restart as a nation. Although victory had been achieved by the Allies, many battles continued.

So it is with Satan. Jesus defeated him on the cross. Paul reminds us of this when he writes, "[Christ] disarmed the rulers and authorities and put them to open shame, by triumphing over them in him" (Colossians 2:15).

Yet, battles continue. The famous Nuremberg trials that saw Nazi leaders tried for war crimes began in the summer of 1945 and lasted over a year. Again, although the Allies had achieved victory, the trials for the leaders of the Third Reich did not come until later. Justice for Satan will come. We see in Revelation that "the devil who had deceived them was thrown into the lake of fire and sulfur where the beast and the false prophet were, and they will be tormented day and night forever and ever" (Revelation 20:10).

How are you doing in the battle? Are you living to honor Jesus? Are you living out the victory we already have in him?

Questions for Day 41
1. Are you living right now in a way that honors Jesus?
2. What are some areas in your life where you struggle and may even be letting Satan have his way?
3. What is a story of victory over temptation you could share to encourage someone else?

Prayer for Day 41
I praise you, Jesus, for your victory over our enemy. Thank you for achieving my freedom from his bondage and oppression. Fill me with your Spirit to live in a way that honors you – to obey you, serve you, and share you with others.

DAY 42
VICTORY OVER DEATH

Mary Magdalene went and announced to the disciples, "I have seen the Lord" (John 20:18).

The First Real Resurrection
As we stated in the Introduction of this book, there really has only been one true resurrection – the resurrection of Jesus. All the other six we've discussed so far were actually resuscitations. The son of the widow at Zarephath, the son of the Shunammite woman, the man who touched Elisha's bones, the son of the widow at Nain, the daughter of Jairus, and Lazarus all went on to die again. They were revived by the power of God. They lived, perhaps for decades after their miraculous moment. However, they would again physically die. But NOT Jesus. He rose again and is alive forevermore.

The Resurrected Body
We don't know all the details, but the Scriptures give us snapshots of what the resurrected body will be like. With Jesus as our prototype, we know a few things. First, the resurrected Jesus was physical. When Jesus showed up to the disciples in his resurrected body, Thomas touched Jesus' hands and side. He felt the physical matter of Jesus' body.

However, in the same scene where Thomas touches Jesus' physical body, Jesus appeared to them without walking through the door. John 20 records how Jesus appears in the midst of the disciples in spite of the doors being closed and locked. So, although physical, the resurrected body evidently has some exceptions to the physics of the natural, fallen creation.

Many people recognize Jesus. When he appears to the disciples, they know who he is. When the disciples see Jesus on the seashore in John 21, they know who he is. However, when Jesus travels on the road to Emmaus, the couple doesn't recognize him until he breaks bread in their home over dinner. Then Jesus vanishes (Luke 24).

Evidence
This great news is the gospel. Jesus died on the cross but rose from the grave and is alive. Here is what is so fascinating about the immediate impact the resurrection had. The apostles and the women who were with them knew Jesus had died. John, Mary, Mary Magdalene, and a couple of others were present while Jesus was on the cross. All of them

were involved following Jesus' death and could confirm that, indeed, the Son of God had died. Yet, decades later, all the apostles, except John, were martyred. How can that be? How can a group of people all be executed for what they believed with not a single one of them recanting or denouncing Jesus?

The answer is simple. They did not die for what they believed. They died for what they knew they saw – a dead man coming out of the tomb alive! And because Jesus lives, they were not afraid. If Jesus conquered death and promised them he would deliver them as well, they had no fear of death.

Today, there is no reason for us to fear death, either. The same Jesus that rose from the dead and made promises to the disciples also makes the same promises to us. Death is not the unbeatable enemy anymore. Death is not the unstoppable force anymore. Jesus has won! Our foe is vanquished. Our eternal life is secure! THIS is what Easter is all about. Happy Easter!

Questions for Day 42
1. How does knowing that Jesus defeated your death make you feel?
2. How does faith in Jesus and his resurrection change your life now?
3. Who else in your life needs to know that Jesus has conquered their death as well?

Prayer for Day 42
Lord Jesus, I praise you that you are alive! You conquered death. You are worthy of all the praise, love, obedience, and devotion I can give you and so much more. Help me this Easter season to share this most amazing news with someone who needs to hear it.

APPENDIX A
RESURRECTION OF MANY SAINTS

And behold, the curtain of the temple was torn in two, from top to bottom. And the earth shook, and the rocks were split. The tombs also were opened. And many bodies of the saints who had fallen asleep were raised, and coming out of the tombs after his resurrection they went into the holy city and appeared to many (Matthew 27:51-53).

Thriller Night?

My (Martin's) parents had told my older brothers that they were to never play the Michael Jackson record when they were out of the house. The 1980s had witnessed Jackson's fame increase with the hit record *Thriller*. My parents were worried that the song "Thriller" would scare me. So, when my parents left one night to go out, my older brothers quickly turned on the song. Guess what? It scared me! I still remember the sound of Vincent Price's eerie laughter and the words to Michael Jackson's iconic hit song:

> Darkness falls across the land
> The midnight hour is close at hand
> Creatures crawl in search of blood
> To terrorize y'all's neighborhood

What a Strange Story!

If you read the Gospels, you will only find the story of dead saints coming back to life after Jesus' resurrection in Matthew's Gospel. It is an eerie story that reminds me a bit of Vincent Price's words. What was going on here and why didn't the other Gospel writers mention this story? What about other historical accounts to this crazy supernatural event? Unfortunately, Matthew is the only one who records this resuscitation event and nothing else is really known about it.

N.T. Wright speaks of this story in his great work: *The Resurrection of the Son of God*. Wright offers four possible solutions to what happened in Matthew. Some of the possibilities Wright puts forward are symbolic, while others require a straightforward, literal reading of the text. Daniel and I both believe this account by Matthew is a literal resuscitation story that demonstrates the power of God over death. As you read Matthew 27, the apostle moves from the crucifixion scene to three days later, when the risen saints appear to many in Jerusalem, and then back to Jesus' death and the Roman Centurion's acknowledgement of Jesus. It is a strange story indeed, but one that demonstrates that some powerful things were going on in Jerusalem.

"The saints who had fallen asleep were raised..."

In Michael Jackson's song, the dead were raised! Price says, "Creatures crawl in search of blood, to terrorize y'all's neighborhood." These "zombies" were apparently in search of blood in the song. In the Gospel of Matthew, the opposite is true. The shed blood of Jesus led to the defeat of death and resurrection power displayed in these risen saints. Many questions are suggested by this account: What did they say? To whom did they appear? How long did they live after they were raised? There are no good answers for these questions.

What we do know is that the future looks good for resurrection. The Scriptures teach us that one day there will be a resurrection of the just and the unjust. John 5:28-29 says, "Do not marvel at this, for an hour is coming when all who are in the tombs will hear his voice and come out, those who have done good to the resurrection of life, and those who have done evil to the resurrection of judgment." Some will receive a body to be eternally destroyed, while others will receive a body like Jesus and live in eternal fellowship with God. This final resurrection will be no mere resuscitation, but a resurrection that lasts forever.

1 Corinthians 15: 53-55 says it best regarding our eternal state, "For this perishable body must put on the imperishable, and this mortal body must put on immortality. When the perishable puts on the imperishable, and the mortal puts on immortality, then shall come to pass the saying that is written: 'Death is swallowed up in victory. O death, where is your victory? O death, where is your sting?'"

APPENDIX B
THE RAISING OF TABITHA

But Peter put them all outside, and knelt down and prayed; and turning to the body he said, "Tabitha, arise." And she opened her eyes, and when she saw Peter she sat up.... And it became known throughout all Joppa, and many believed in the Lord (Acts 9:40, 42).

New Leadership?

In most world religions, once the founder of the religion died, he would be succeeded by a family member or protégé. For example, in Islam, when Muhammad died (AD 632) there was a great dispute over who Muhammad's successor would be. Many named his friend, Abu Bakr, the new caliph. This group of Abu Bakr supporters were and are known as the Sunni Muslims. Another group supported Muhammad's cousin Ali as the new caliph. This group was and is known as Shi'a Muslims. That is not the case in Christianity. When Jesus died on the cross, he did not name someone to succeed him as Messiah. He was and is the only Messiah; and there was no need to name a successor, because Jesus lives. He came out of the tomb alive.

The historical account of Tabitha affirms that Jesus needed no successor. Although many see Peter as Jesus' successor, Peter never made such a claim. When Peter raised Tabitha from the dead, no one said, "Praise be to Peter!" No! Verse 42 is very clear that many people believed in *the Lord*! They trusted in the living Jesus who continued his work through the indwelling Holy Spirit.

Peter Prayed

Had Peter himself been the Messiah, he may not have needed to pray before performing this amazing miracle. Many times, Jesus simply spoke or acted in doing mighty works. When raising Lazarus, Jesus admits in his prayer he was only praying so the people gathered would know the Father would hear him (John 11:41). Peter was not the Messiah; he had to pray. He had to tap into the source of the resurrection power - Jesus.

Jesus Continued

In his book *Jesus Continued*, pastor and author J.D. Greear describes how the Holy Spirit continues the work of Jesus in us and through us. Peter is the living example of this truth as he performs the miracle that only God can do – bringing the dead back to life.

However, as in the six resuscitations prior to Jesus' resurrection, Tabitha would die again. But being a believer in Jesus, as indicated by the author of Acts (Luke) referring to her as a "disciple," full of "good works and charity" (Acts 9:36), Tabitha is guaranteed the resurrection of Jesus, as are all of us who trust in him.

APPENDIX C
SLEEPING EUTYCHUS

And a young man named Eutychus, sitting at the window, sank into a deep sleep as Paul talked still longer. And being overcome by sleep, he fell down from the third story and was taken up dead. But Paul went down and bent over him, and taking him in his arms, said, "Do not be alarmed, for his life is in him." … And they took the youth away alive, and were not a little comforted (Acts 20:9-10, 12).

Sleeping Hazard

When I (Daniel) was a freshman (a "plebe") at West Point, I struggled to stay awake in chemistry class. Three days a week, I would go to chemistry right after lunch and battle the fog of sleepiness. Usually, my solution was to stand up in class. My professor was a colonel and head of the entire chemistry department, so I knew I had better not disrespect him by falling asleep in his class. One day, the unthinkable happened. As the heavy fog of sleepiness moved in, I stood up in class and leaned up against the wall behind me. Then, I actually fell asleep standing up. To this day, I'm not sure what awakened me. Was it the sense that I was beginning to fall over to my side or was it the flying chalkboard eraser hitting me in the chest? All I know was that as I opened my eyes, I was able to catch myself from falling over, simultaneously realizing I had chalk residue all over my uniform – which meant much hazing by upperclassmen as I walked back to the barracks. I wasn't dead, but I sure had some suffering coming!

This one particular Sunday, the apostle Paul was preaching in the city of Troas. He preached a very long time. Acts 20:7 says his speech lasted until midnight! This lengthy homily proved to be too much for the young Eutychus as he succumbed to the thick fog of sleepiness.

The Need to Wake Up

So much of our lives are pictured in this simple yet miraculous story of Eutychus. Distractions and pursuits in life can lull us into spiritual sleep. We can become so enamored with sports or hobbies or entertainment that we begin to doze off in our relationship with Jesus. Our careers can take center stage in our lives, causing us to inadvertently relax our walks with Jesus. Like Eutychus, we don't really intend to go to sleep. But drowsiness still sets in and before we know it, we're asleep.

At some point in Paul's message – maybe after sermon point 41 – Eutychus begins to drift into unconsciousness. The next thing he knows, his parents are taking him away alive. No doubt there would have been quite a stir over this boy who died and then came back to life. Eutychus had been jolted out of his slumber and scrambled to understand what had happened.

If you're sleeping in your walk with Jesus or drowsy in your faith, our prayer for you is that the Lord, in his kindness, would awaken you, fresh and new. We pray for you the words of Jesus to the church at Sardis in Revelation 3:2-3a, "Wake up! Strengthen what remains and is about to die, for I have not found your deeds complete in the sight of my God. Remember, therefore, what you have received and heard; obey it, and repent."

ABOUT THE AUTHORS

Daniel Carr has been lead pastor of Canaan Baptist Church in St. Louis since 2012. Daniel is a graduate of Southern Baptist Theological Seminary and the United States Military Academy. He is married to Tara, and they have seven children.

Martin Winslow has served as pastor of families and missions for Canaan Baptist Church in St. Louis since 2017. Martin is a graduate of Midwestern Baptist Theological Seminary. Martin and his wife, Amy, have five children.

Carr and Winslow are also the authors of *The Seventh Birthday: An Advent Devotional for Families*, available at Amazon.com.